THE RESCUE DOG

A Guide to Successful Re-Homing

Vanessa Stead and Ann Stead

THE CROWOOD PRESS

First published in 2010 by
The Crowood Press Ltd
Ramsbury, Marlborough
Wiltshire SN8 2HR

www.crowood.com

British Library Cataloguing-in-Publication Data
A catalogue record for this book is available from the British Library.

ISBN 978 1 84797 180 7

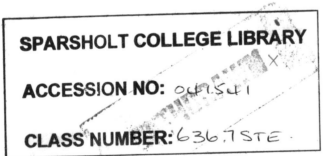
Typeset by Sharon Kemmett, Isis Design
Printed and bound in India by Replika Press Pvt Ltd

CONTENTS

INTRODUCTION

You have already made two major decisions: you have decided to get a dog, and you have decided to re-home one from a rescue organization.

THE RESCUE DOG

Many people believe that rescue dogs are troubled, traumatized strays with long-lasting problems. While this view may be justified for some, in reality there is a tremendous amount of variation between the dogs in re-homing centres all over the world. The dogs are there for a large and varied number of reasons, most of which have little to do with the actual dog. The most common reasons are extremely relevant in the selection of a suitable companion.

Before you even step through the door of the re-homing centre, you need to have thought about what sort of dog you are looking for.

There are many reasons why a dog might enter a re-homing centre:

- It may be a stray, found wandering the streets by a dog warden.
- It may have been rescued from deliberate human neglect and cruelty.
- Its owners may have divorced and can no longer look after it.
- Its owner may have become ill or died.
- Its family may have run into debt, lost their jobs or their homes and can no longer afford to keep it.
  These dogs often come with a full repertoire of tricks they can do, as well as their favourite bed and blanket.
- Many 'accidental' matings result in puppies whose owners struggle to find home for them; these puppies may end up in a re-homing centre.
- There are also dogs that have become 'too old', and may even have been cast aside to make way for a younger model.
- Some owners cannot cope with their dog's behaviour – but a dog who is a problem for one family may be another's characterful companion.

The Advantages of Re-Homing a Rescue Dog

Where better to start your search for your ideal dog, the dog most suitable to your lifestyle and requirements, than amongst the thousands in re-homing centres looking for a home. When you look down a row of kennels you become aware of the variety in appearance, age, size, activity level and character between dogs. From pure-bred dogs to unfathomable cross-breeds, the huge diversity offers you a fantastic selection from which to choose the most suitable companion for your family. During your search you will have the additional benefit of trained staff to help you find the 'ideal match' and perfect companion.

If you have set your heart on a particular breed it is possible to find one in many of the re-homing centres around the country. However, there are also breed-specific rescue organizations that concentrate on a single breed and are often associated with a breed club. Most breed-specific rescue organizations do not have dedicated kennels and may use foster homes, or may re-home directly from the previous owner.

If you are in search of a dog to suit a specific age group, from children to the elderly, you can find one in a re-homing centre. Many families with children are in search of a dog to complete their home. The wide range of dogs – from puppies to seniors and quite literally every age group in between – means that you can find the right dog for you.

Dog ownership has been found to be very beneficial to the elderly. A study of 938 people aged sixty-five and over found that those who owned pets had fewer visits to the doctor than those who did not. Dogs offered additional advantages such as reducing stress, and providing companionship and an object of attachment, which is associated with better mental health and a higher sense of morale. Feeling secure is particularly important for the elderly, and this is provided much more by a dog than any other pet[1]. Many of the dogs in re-homing centres would make excellent companions for the elderly, ticking all the right boxes with regard to characteristics.

Many professionals are involved in ensuring the rescue dog is ready for re-homing, and the majority of re-homing centres vaccinate. Some rescue organizations, such as the Dog's Trust, also neuter their dogs. Furthermore they will help you resolve any initial difficulties by offering training tips and other advice.

Re-homing a dog from a rescue organization is a fantastic thing to do from an ethical perspective. Giving a home to one of the thousands of dogs in need is a huge step in helping reduce the problem of unwanted dogs. You are also undoubtedly making a life-changing difference to a living creature when you re-home a dog that has been selected specifically for your family.

While there are many differences between rescue dogs, there is one thing that unites them: they all need to be given the chance of a better life. Successfully re-homing a rescue dog can be a rewarding experience in itself, but it has yet another wonderful side effect: you may just find the friend of a lifetime.

An intelligent, calm and friendly lurcher puppy, which adores people: a perfect family companion.

1 MAKING THE DECISION

There are many decisions to be made during the process of re-homing a rescue dog, and organizing your thoughts, feelings and requirements is a good place to start. In the first part of this chapter we will take you through the decision-making process, helping you to focus gradually on the characteristics of the dog that will suit you and your family. We will then lead you through the re-homing procedure so you know what to expect and are prepared for this serious commitment.

WHICH BREED OF DOG?

If you decide to re-home a dog belonging to a particular breed, then to some extent you know what to expect, as pure-breed dogs have been bred for specific purposes. Therefore we strongly advise you to research the physical and mental characteristics that are most prominent in your preferred breed. The Kennel Club breed standards are an excellent place to start, as these cover aspects such as size, behaviour, health concerns and even life expectancy. This will give you an insight into the mental, physical and functional nature of that breed. However, we must

A 'SECOND' THOUGHT

All dogs to some degree or another can cause mess in your home. They just can't help their paws attracting mud, nor resist rolling in smelly substances, often the smellier the better! Some dogs can't avoid dribbling water from their bowls all over the house – and they can't help the occasional toilet accident when you have been out a little longer than you should have been.

This is the reality of owning a dog, and if any of this sounds intolerable, you need to consider whether your priority is a tidy home or a happy dog. Of course you can have both, but it may well require more frequent housework. This is one aspect of re-homing a dog that you really must consider before you sign on the dotted line.

This dog is making himself very comfortable, though his muddy paws are making a mess on the sofa.

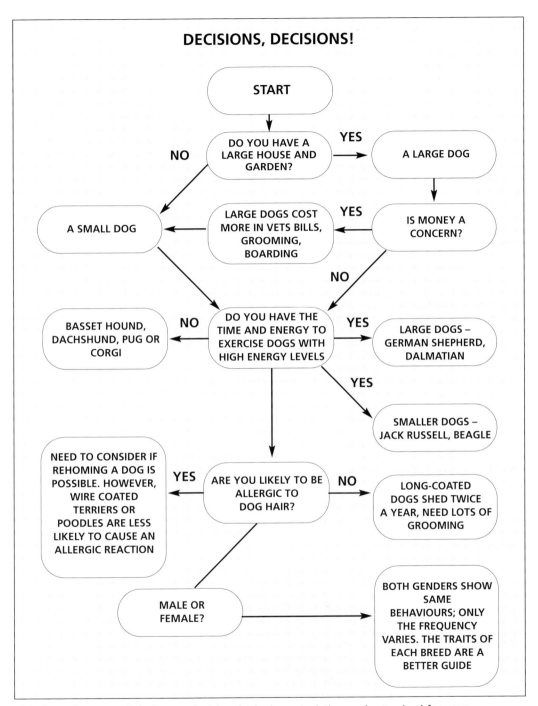

DECISIONS, DECISIONS!

This flow diagram will help you decide which characteristics are best suited for your circumstances. You can discuss them with the re-homing centre, and your notes will help when filling out the forms most centres use to facilitate a good match.

emphasize that every dog is an individual, which means that temperament and character may vary greatly even within a highly selected breed.

If you are interested in re-homing a cross-breed dog, determining which breed of dog he is crossed with can be very useful. It can be a great deal of fun and may keep you guessing, but if your guesses are correct you will have some idea of what to expect of him.

BEHAVIOURAL TENDENCIES

There is a common perception that males tend to be adventurous and need strong handling, and that females tend to be more docile. The truth is far from simple, and there is enormous individual variation within the sexes. Research has found that both genders show the same behaviours; it is only the frequency that varies.

A dog's gender will not therefore enable you to predict how it is going to behave, and basing your expectations of an individual dog solely on its gender, or any other particular trait, will undoubtedly lead to misconceptions. Critically these may affect how you behave towards the dog, and could be detrimental to the relationship you have with him. The story of Ollie shows how this can happen.

Understanding Ollie

Ollie was a one-year-old, male blue merle collie, found as a stray. He was re-homed by a young couple who had many friends with dogs and therefore wanted Ollie to socialize regularly. Ollie had been neutered only a fortnight before, and while he was at the re-homing centre he was extremely sociable and loved playing with male and female dogs both neutered and un-neutered. He had been kennelled with a female lurcher and had

You may find both pure-breed and cross-breed dogs looking for a home. Before you reach this point do some homework as to the breed of dog most suitable for your family.

never been a concern with other dogs.

Ollie's new owners knew his background and decided to develop a method of handling based on his recently neutered male status. They decided that Ollie was likely to be dominant, headstrong, trying and challenging both in and out of the home. They had never had a dog before and were determined that their new dog should be as well behaved as possible.

Ollie's first outing was a trip to the stable yard where the couple's friends were waiting with their dogs. When Ollie caught sight of the dogs he became very excited and eager to make friends, so started to whimper and give a few high-pitched barks. The couple were extremely worried by this and were certain that Ollie was displaying dominant behaviour, particularly as he was pulling on the lead. They punished him by jerking the lead and shouting.

Ollie barked louder and pulled more intently. He was punished again, and at this point the friends brought their dogs closer. Ollie continued to jump up and down on the lead, barking loudly and thus convincing his owners that he was challenging them.

Ollie was now desperate, confused, and becoming very stressed by the whole affair. When he reached forwards to say 'Hello' to a spaniel belonging to one of the friends, his owner tightened the lead, so he couldn't respond normally when the spaniel jumped up on his back. The formerly well socialized, confident Ollie, who had gone through this many times before, would normally have just given a growl to tell the spaniel to back off; but now, recently punished, confused and anxious, instead of uttering just a low-key warning, he delivered a more aggressive snap towards the spaniel's nose. This

resulted in further punishment, and made the new owners even more convinced that they were correct in their assessment of him as a dominant, aggressive male dog.

The reality was sadly very different, and their incorrect assumptions, together with inappropriate handling, merely set poor Ollie up for failure.

Respect Individuality

Knowledge and information about your new dog is essential when starting your relationship, but use this carefully as each dog is an individual. The young couple who re-homed Ollie were set to fail from the start due to their incorrect assumption that as a recently neutered male he needed very firm handling. If you respect a dog's individuality, and make sure you do not focus solely on factors such as gender, it will be more likely that you will make a success of re-homing a rescue dog.

NEUTERING

The majority of re-homing centres neuter their dogs before they are ready to be re-homed. Others give out neutering vouchers for dogs that cannot be neutered before they are taken home. Many of the re-homing centres will schedule in follow-up calls and visits to ensure the operation has been carried out, for the simple reason that there are far more unwanted dogs than there are homes for them. By preventing conception there will be fewer dogs around to be abandoned, given up or even destroyed.

For those of you who are uncertain about male and female differences, it has been established that the traits differentiating the sexes tend to be altered by castration in 50–60 per cent of dogs[3]. Even if this were not the case, neutering offers important health advantages.

The female dog is 'designed' to have two pregnancies a year. If she does not conceive, she may suffer a false pregnancy following a season, making her feel miserable and uncomfortable, which could lead to behavioural problems. What is more, it is estimated that up to half of the unneutered female population suffers from a womb infection called pyometra, which can be fatal. Neutering not only removes this risk, but if done early also protects against mammary cancer.

Male dogs can also be protected by neutering, as this removes the risk of testicular cancer and significantly reduces the likelihood of tumours and later prostate problems.

MORE THAN ONE DOG?

In answer to the question whether it is preferable to have more than one dog, it depends on the particular dogs you are considering, and your reason for wanting another dog.

If you watch dogs playing together, it is clear why it can be beneficial for them to have a companion of their own species. They enjoy a good rough and tumble, and often use their mouths and teeth in a manner we would be foolish to emulate. This sort of play can be very intense, and it is a constant surprise that both parties not only escape injury, but seem to be having so much fun. Social interaction is very important for the large majority of dogs, and it can have huge benefits to both the behaviour and welfare of the dog, especially in the kennel environment.

Dogs learn extremely effectively by observing others, and it is important to bear this in mind when considering re-homing another. Your new dog may well learn undesirable behaviour from the dog you have already, so you may just be doubling your troubles.

Reasons for adding another dog	How you think this will help	Possible outcomes	Suggestions
My year-old collie cross is very sociable and would benefit from another dog.	Companionship, play friend and second family dog.	Suitable dog will act as a play friend, and companion and a loved member of the family.	Look for a dog that is friendly and sociable with humans and other dogs alike.
My two-year-old labrador needs more exercise and I haven't time to take him on walks.	He will play with the second dog so they will exercise each other.	The second dog may not necessarily help your current dog to become more active. Your new dog will also require walking and will potentially become problematic if he is not adequately exercised.	If you don't have time for one dog, two dogs are going to stretch you. It is important to focus on your dog and find an alternative solution. A dog walker could be a consideration.
I want to stop my three-year-old male poodle from patrolling along our fence and barking at our neighbour.	A new dog would not know to do this and would distract our poodle when he tries.	Dogs learn from each other through observational learning. It is possible that a new dog could learn the same behaviour.	If you have any concerns it is important to rectify these before taking on another dog. If you do not it is likely that you may have double the trouble when a new dog arrives.
To help my nine-year-old German shepherd male overcome his severe fear and aggression towards other dogs.	A new dog will encourage him to become sociable with other dogs as he has never lived with a dog before.	Conflict between the two dogs is likely, and may lead to further aggression and injury. 'Flooding' the German shepherd with what he is frightened of may lead to emotional and physical shut-down and a very miserable dog.	Seek professional advice. The German shepherd may require behaviour modification training to help him overcome his fears. It is possible he will be happier as an only dog.
My fifteen-year-old female spaniel seems to be suffering from the loss of our sixteen-year-old Staffordshire bull terrier cross.	Adding a puppy will rejuvenate her and bring her back to how she was six years ago when we got our Staffordshire bull terrier. Although she cannot walk far for medical reasons, a puppy will help her to feel happier and be more active.	Puppies are active and playful, but this may not be in the best interest of your elderly spaniel. As she has physical ailments, a puppy may be too much for her. Nor will this situation benefit the puppy.	Seek veterinary advice to assess if your current dog could cope with the introduction of a new companion. If she is mentally and physically capable, consider an older, less active dog that is not likely to jump on her or make her unhappy.

It is essential to assess each dog's individual needs to see if a companion dog would be right for him. A second dog could make a significant difference to your current dog's emotional and physical state and wellbeing, and this could be positive or negative, either of which could affect you and your family. If your dogs are happy and content without conflict or concern, it is much more likely that you will feel the same.

Choosing Responsibly

A great deal of care is needed in choosing a suitable second dog. Our responses remain the same whether a dog is male or female, but a dog's response to another male and his response to a female may be quite different. While gender in a single dog is not a particular concern, it is a significant factor in successfully re-homing a companion for your current dog. A male dog may tolerate the instigation and continuation of rough play from female dogs, but he may rarely accept it from the males. It is advisable to re-home dogs of the opposite sex to reduce possible conflict issues, however some dogs of the same sex can become the very best of friends. It depends greatly on the individual dogs you are considering.

It is important to treat both dogs equally, as research shows that they have the ability to recognize when the other is getting preferential treatment. In a study at the University of Vienna, pairs of dogs were given commands to place their paws in the experimenter's hands, and when they obeyed, they were given a reward. When one dog wasn't given a reward for obeying, and the other dog in the pair was, the unrewarded dog would refuse to respond to the repeated commands.

Whilst we cannot claim that the unrewarded dog felt this was unfair, it does show that he recognized that a rule had been broken and that his own place in the 'game' needed to be re-established. Therefore each dog should have his own food, water bowl, lead and collar, as well as toys. You will need to give both dogs individual attention to ensure the attachment you have with both of them continues to be secure.

Introducing a new dog needs sensitive handling as it is quite possible for one dog to simply dislike another. You should, therefore, ask the re-homing centre if they can arrange for the two dogs to meet in a calm environment away from the kennel area so that you can see if they are going to be a good match.

REPLACING A LOVED ONE

One of the most painful situations a dog owner must face is the loss of a canine friend; the grief this generates is often as great as the loss of a relative, and leaves a huge hole in daily life. You constantly think you have seen your pet out of the corner of your eye, and the house feels empty when you return home. When you are ready and in a position to do so you may want to get another dog. The grief you feel may make it difficult to look down the line at a re-homing centre – but remember you are not only helping yourself, you are also offering a chance of happiness to a dog in need.

Although you may find a dog that looks identical to your old friend, it is unlikely he will have an identical character or personality. To avoid disappointment and potential resentment on both sides, it is best to approach your visit to the re-homing centre with a fresh eye.

It is important not be inflexible in your choice, especially when you are hoping to replace a beloved pet. Dogs of a particular breed obviously look the same, but they are all individuals and may not fill the place left by your old friend. There are many reasons why a pairing might not work, and the re-homing centre has the knowledge and experience to make a sound decision. Trust them.

Replacing a loved one can be such an emotional and difficult thing to do. If you feel you are ready to re-home a new dog after the loss of another, then take time to find the right individual. The loss may have left a large gap in your life, but take care to select your next dog for his temperament and suitability rather than for his similarity to your previous dog.

THE RESPONSIBLE DECISION

A family with a five-year-old daughter came to the centre where Vanessa was working. They had had experience with collies for over ten years, but had lost their old collie a few weeks earlier; they now wanted to meet a new dog that had recently arrived from Ireland. They had seen him on the website, and he looked exactly like their previous dog. He was a one-year-old stray, and was very nervous, reacting with fear to both noise and movement. Vanessa was certain he would be unable to cope with a five-year-old used to playing with her dog as she would with her human friends. This collie boy was quiet, shut down and definitely not ready, and maybe would never be ready for this type of home environment.

Two facts prevented this potential offer of a home: in the first place there was no evidence that the collie was sociable with children, and this was compounded by the fact that he was extremely nervous. It would have been very irresponsible to have allowed him to go to a home with such a young child as there was no way to safety-test him with young children.

Vanessa therefore had to turn down this kind offer of a home. Such decisions can be very upsetting and difficult to understand, but in such situations the re-homing centre is simply trying to facilitate a suitable match.

2 WHERE TO GO AND WHAT TO EXPECT

The number of rescue organizations throughout the UK and Ireland is vast, and many of these have a re-homing centre where you can select a suitable dog. Some rescue organizations are 'breed specific', so if you are in search of a pure breed dog then you may still find your perfect companion here. Many re-homing centres have their policies, details of their opening days and visiting hours, as well as information about their available dogs, all listed on their websites, so you can do some ground-work about these from the comfort of your home before your visit. However, although the majority of re-homing centres try to keep their website up to date, things can change a great deal in just a day – every time the phone rings it could be another owner on the end of the line asking the centre to accept their dog for re-homing. It is therefore useful to bear in mind the following three points:

- Just because you can't see 'your' dog on their website doesn't mean he isn't at the re-homing centre. A great deal can change in a day. Check the status quo with a quick phone call.
- Introduce yourself and get to know the kennel staff so they can help you find the right dog and contact you if a suitable candidate becomes available.

- Try to stay patient, and don't give up! There are so many dogs looking for homes, each time you inquire you increase your chances of finding 'your' dog.

WHAT TO EXPECT

Re-homing centres do an important job, and the large majority of them set high standards in animal welfare. It is very expensive to run a rescue organization, particularly a re-homing centre, therefore many have set fees, while others ask for a donation when you re-home a dog. Before you waste either your own time or that of the re-homing centre, it is worthwhile asking about fees, as they can be well over £100. If you are asked for an excessive amount you should check if the re-homing centre is a registered charity accountable for their funds. However, a high fee may cover charges for vaccinations, micro-chipping, neutering and flea and worm treatment, most of which you will have to have done anyway.

Most re-homing centres require a person to be over eighteen years old before they will allow them to re-home a dog, and you will certainly be asked to complete an application form. Do not expect to take home the dog you like there and then; this is not like buying a

You may find your emotions run away with you when you walk past so many lovely dogs needing homes.

Collies in particular find kennel life difficult to cope with. This collie clearly wants to leave the confines of his kennel.

Some dogs, such as this springer spaniel, appear to be patiently waiting for someone to take them out of their kennel.

new hamster. Re-homing centres need to be sure that the dog is going to a suitable home, which could mean that you are required to visit the dog several times before taking him.

This is especially true if you have children, because they will want to see that the dog is calm and confident around your child, and vice versa. Some have a policy not to place rescue dogs with owners who have any children under a certain age, usually five years old. This rule is there for your family's safety, and however unfair such a restriction may seem when you are intent on a specific dog, please remember that these precautions are responsible and necessary.

Many rescue organizations make neutering a condition of re-homing, while others have the operation carried out before the dog can go home. In view of the high number of unwanted dogs, this is responsible behaviour and, as discussed earlier, there are additional health benefits for the dog, especially later in life.

VISITING THE RE-HOMING CENTRE

We know you will want to make a good impression, and that can be achieved by showing you mean business. Wear comfortable shoes and bring wet weather clothes as it very likely you will be outside at some point in your visit. Wear items that you don't mind getting dirty, and trousers or jeans that allow you to bend or kneel down and will protect your legs against scratches. Many of the dogs will be very pleased to see you when you come to visit, and show this by jumping up on you. It is certainly best to be prepared.

When you plan your visit to the re-homing centre allow yourself plenty of time to look round. Obviously the more individual kennels there are, the more time you will need: for example, if there are over fifty kennels leave yourself an hour or two. It gives a poor impression of your commitment if you seem to be in a rush to go somewhere else. You will also need time to talk to the carers, who can be extremely useful as they know the dogs personally and can tell you those all-important, extra details.

At this stage you should leave any other dogs or pets at home, as your presence alone is enough to raise the general stress levels of the residents. If you are in search of a companion for a current dog, leave him at home for the first visit as this will leave you free to focus all your attention on the dogs before you. You will be required to bring your current dog at a later stage to meet the dog you are interested in, to ensure they are a good match.

THE KENNEL ENVIRONMENT

It is important to consider how dogs react to the kennel environment, as this will help you understand many of the behaviours you may see. But first let us take a brief look into the world of the kennels from the dog's eye view.

It is important to emphasize that many of the dogs in re-homing centres are not seen at their best because the very nature of the environment is stressful. The first thing visitors are likely to notice about some re-homing centres is the excessive noise, which can make some people want to go straight back home. Although it is the dogs themselves causing the noise, they, too, can be very stressed by it. Fore-

A dog's eye view: the light is blocked out by the figure at the kennel front, and this is enough to cause additional stress and fear for some dogs. Never put fingers or hands through the bars as kennelled dogs could become anxious very easily.

warned is forearmed, so be prepared for this, and try to bear it for the amount of time necessary to look carefully at the dogs.

Many people find this environment distressing – but remember, these dogs are the lucky ones as they are being fed and cared for. Meanwhile thousands of others are roaming the streets, or in homes with owners unable to care for them, or, in the worst case scenario, with owners who mistreat them. An hour looking around a re-homing centre may be just enough time to meet the perfect dog for you.

Appearances can certainly be deceptive, so it is vital to remember that the kennel environment will be influencing the behaviour of every dog in some way. Kennelled dogs are often anxious due to a number of factors, not least of which is the presence of so many other dogs. A study conducted in 1998 that compared dogs able to see what was going on outside their kennel, with dogs denied that privilege, revealed that the former group spent significantly more of their time at the front of the pen (in a position to see other dogs and people passing) than the latter group (87.7 per cent versus 24.6 per cent)[5].

The down side of this is that many re-homing centres have no alternative than to walk unfamiliar or potentially aggressive dogs past each other in the kennels. This contributes significantly to increasing the stress levels of the dogs that spend most of their time at the front of the kennel.

Many of the dogs find it difficult to relax because their brain is constantly alert. Some may also suffer from sleep deprivation. It would therefore be unfair to base your judgment on any dog exclusively from your viewing of him in the kennel environment. The behaviour you will witness is a window into the dog's physical, mental and emotional state, and if you just stop to consider why the dog is behaving in this way, this will ensure that you do not reject a dog that may in fact be very suitable for your family. If you are interested in any of the dogs, contact the kennel staff and find out more about them.

The most commonly observed behaviour is excessive barking, although some dogs become depressed and listless while others become overactive. There are also some dogs who find kennel life so difficult to cope with that they exhibit stereotypical behaviour (behaviours that are excessively repeated, compulsive and without an obvious purpose) such as tail chasing, circling, whirling round and bouncing repeatedly off the kennel walls[6]. Stress is rife among kennelled dogs, and can be caused by a number of factors.

This dog displays stress and frustration as it watches another dog walking past her kennel (its nose can just be seen at left). Such dogs may appear aggressive in these circumstances, but this does not reflect their 'true' nature.

SIGNALS BEHIND BARS

The following section is a photographic representation of the behaviours and expressions typical of dogs suffering different emotions and stress levels caused by incarceration in the kennel environment.

The Stressed Dog
- Facial ridges and mouth rigid and open: This expression indicates tension and stress, and in little Tommy's case is accompanied by high-pitched barking.
- Pawing at the kennel: This behaviour indicates that the dog has a strong desire to leave and is finding confinement difficult. It is often accompanied by frustration and additional stress.
- Erratic jumping up: Tommy here is jumping up repeatedly, and this behaviour intensifies every time a dog walks past his kennel. Jumping up to the kennel front is common in kennelled dogs, and may be accompanied by other rapid movements such as pacing, wall jumping and spinning.

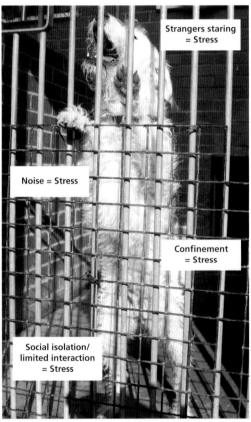

Strangers staring = Stress

Noise = Stress

Confinement = Stress

Social isolation/ limited interaction = Stress

Stress can be caused by a number of factors within the kennel environment. Some re-homing centres are more stressful than others, and this is greatly influenced by kennel design and layout.

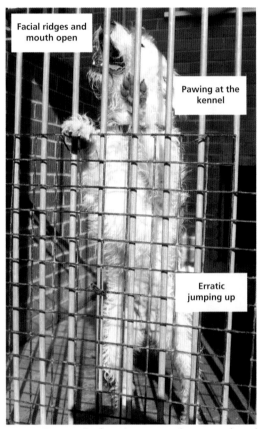

Facial ridges and mouth open

Pawing at the kennel

Erratic jumping up

Tommy is showing several stress-related behaviours as he jumps up at the kennel front.

These behaviours can become stereotypical in nature as the dog finds it more difficult to cope with the stress.

- Tongue held out low down and wider at the bottom: This is a helpful signal, and different from the dog panting to cool down. The tongue is lower and wider at the bottom, and held with more tension than the hot but relaxed dog's tongue[7].
- Tense ears held to the side: The ears are rigid and held awkwardly, and match Flash's 'zoned out' expression.
- Facial ridges around the mouth: The lips and cheeks have clear ridges all around, made more visible by Flash's raised and tense top lip. These ridges are visible right through to the cheeks where there are further, smaller lines.
- Tense body and leg stance: The legs and body are rigid and tense with an almost 'wooden' appearance.

Collie-type dogs find the kennel environment particularly difficult to cope with. Collies are very active, intelligent dogs, neither of which helps them to cope when confined behind bars for many hours a day. As a result, many of them exhibit signs of stress and stereotypical behaviours. Remember these behaviours may be largely situational, and you should find out more about the dog before passing him by, especially if you feel a collie could be the right dog for you.

The Uncertain Dog
- Avoidant: Reluctant to approach; the dog may walk away but then turn back again.

Tense ears, held out to side

Tongue far out, wider at the bottom

Facial ridges round mouth

Tense body and leg stance

Flash is showing the stressed facial expression, typical of many collies in the kennel environment.

Avoidant

Barking at a distance

A small male terrier demonstrating avoidant behaviour and a very worried stance.

- Barking at a distance: This may be a learnt behaviour to keep people at a distance, which also encourages them to keep walking.

The little terrier on page 21 had only been in the kennels for a day when this photograph was taken, so he is still a little unsure. This behaviour reduced dramatically after a day, but it could reoccur when somebody he does not know approaches.

- Ears back, held out to the side: The ears are held in a rigid, almost awkward

Ears back, held out to the side

Constant eye contact, wide eyes

Tight lips

On the back foot

Dylan is showing conflicting emotions: 'I would like to approach you but maybe I should back away.'

manner with a great deal of tension. They fit Dylan's conflicting emotions perfectly.

- Tight lips: Dylan has extremely tight lips in the photograph, and the skin around his mouth is tense and tight. This gives him a flattened chin and rigid jaw where his top and bottom teeth are closed together tightly.
- On the back foot: Dylan is displaying inconsistent body language; his front paws are pointed in different directions and his stance is wide. One paw is directed towards the kennel front and the other angled away. This will enable him to make a rapid retreat if he feels it is necessary. This photograph shows a dog that is definitely unsure.
- Constant eye contact and wide eyes: Wide eyes allow Dylan to gain as much visual information as he can, and along with his constant watching, reveals his need to 'keep an eye' on us to make it easier for him to react quickly and move away.

The Happy and Relaxed Dog
- Soft eyes: Rodney's soft eyes are rounded, not wide, and he is without frown lines in the forehead area.
- Ears held naturally and loose: This reflects Rodney's relaxed and calm emotional state at the time this photograph was taken. There is no tension in the ears, so they fall naturally to the side.
- Wagging tail: Rodney's tail is at 'half mast', relaxed and wagging, which contributes to the softness of his posture.
- Relaxed mouth: Rodney's mouth is relaxed and partially open, the lips are relaxed, and there are very few tension lines in the mouth and face area.

Ears held naturally loose and relaxed

Wagging tail

Soft eyes

Relaxed mouth

Confident and relaxed posture

Rodney is quite happy and relaxed having his photo taken.

- Confident and relaxed posture: The body posture is confident as he approaches the kennel run directly without any attempt to back away.

FINDING THE COMPATIBLE DOG

You are now mentally prepared to visit a re-homing centre knowing that many of the dogs will be anxious and, therefore, not behaving as they would out of this environment. You should also be aware of your own behaviour: staring and silence or speaking in a gruff, deep voice is likely to make the dogs even more anxious or fearful. Try to keep your voice neutral and calm, as dogs are more likely to associate such vocal tones with positive rather than threatening situations.

Physical attraction is very important for humans, so don't feel you are being superficial if you base your initial choice on looks, as it is a logical starting point. Whatever the basis of your initial choice, you must also find out from the carers everything you can about the dog you are interested in.

There have been several behaviour tests devised to help you to find a compatible dog. We have refrained from providing one, as no test is foolproof, and in the hands of a novice such a test could be positively dangerous. For example, seeing how a dog responds to being stroked through the bars of his kennel may work for someone sensitive to canine body language, but equally it could lead to lost fingers if the signals are misjudged.

This is not to suggest that rescue dogs are dangerous, just that a dog behind bars is likely to feel vulnerable and defensive, and that can lead to uncharacteristic behaviour. By far the safest and most effective way to gain information about a dog at a re-homing centre is to ask the staff what you would like to know.

The X Factor

You may have prepared yourself, conducted homework about the different breeds, worked out your budget and planned how a new dog is going to fit into your life. You may even have armed yourself with a list of ideal characteristics.

Then you come face to face with a dog that does not conform in any way to your

Questions to ask	Why the answer to these questions are important	Misconceptions
How long has the dog been in a kennel environment at the re-homing centre?	If the dog has been in the re-homing centre for some time, the kennel staff will have got to know him well. They therefore will be able to give you some helpful information about his characteristics and behaviour.	If a dog has been in rescue for a long time (over a year), it does not necessarily mean there is anything wrong with him. Although some dogs struggle to find homes because they have required further training, other long-term residents may not have had the luck to be chosen. Find out more before you reject a dog because he has been there for some time.
What is his background? Was he a stray? How many homes has he had? Has he been returned to the kennels and if so why? Why did his previous owners part with him?	Details about his past can help you to understand his behaviour and to know what to expect.	If the re-homing centre does not have a detailed background about the dog you are interested in, this does not necessarily mean that he is 'problem' dog.
Is he sociable with children? Is he sociable with other dogs? Is he sociable with people? Is he sociable with other animals, e.g. cats?	These questions should relate to your specific circumstances. If you have a cat at home but no children living with you or visiting regularly, then finding a dog who is sociable with cats may be more of a priority than an individual fully sociable with children.	If the re-homing centre has no history about the dog you are interested in, care must be taken when making your choice. Find out if they have conducted any assessments of the dog that may give you vital information about whether or not he is a suitable candidate.
Has the dog's behaviour been assessed? What are the results of the assessment? Does he have any behaviour concerns?	Many re-homing centres assess their dogs' behaviour when they arrive. These assessments may examine elements of his behaviour to help you answer many of the questions you may have. The results of these will help you to discover the right dog for your family.	Just because the re-homing centre does not carry out formal assessments does not mean they are unable to judge a dog's temperament. They may be able to answer many of your questions just through the insight they have gained about him while he has been at the re-homing centre.

Insight into a dog's character, requirements and behaviour will help you decide if he is suitable, and to know what to expect from him, essential for a successful re-homing.

IS HE HOUSE TRAINED?

House training is an important consideration for every owner, and the re-homing centre staff may struggle to give you a definite answer as to whether or not the dog you are interested in is fully house trained. They may certainly be able to give you an idea of what to expect, but it is important to be realistic and to consider that you may need to conduct some training with your new dog when he arrives home.

Many dogs are clean in their kennels and will continue to be so in their new homes. Others that are clean in kennels may relapse as a result of the disruption and uncertainty they undergo when going to a new home. There are also dogs that have never lived in a home before, so they may not understand that they are supposed to 'perform' in a particular place, simply because they have never been taught.

The best way to approach this phase of re-homing is to assume that your new dog is not house trained. Then you will be prepared for some additional training if it turns out he is not, and pleasantly surprised if he is.

ideal, but he has the X factor – that certain something that touches you though you can't identify it, which tells you this is the dog for you – and amazingly he seems to feel the same.

PREPARING FOR RE-HOMING

The first thing is to have a serious chat with a member of staff about the physical and emotional needs of the dog in question. Then go home and think about it rationally. A young dog could be with you for twelve years or more. Look at your reasons for opting for the characteristics on your list, and work out how much adjustment you would need to make to your life in order to accommo-date this new dog.

If the physical and emotional needs of both you and the dog can be met, then move on to the next stage towards re-homing.

Once you have chosen a dog, waste no time in applying to re-home him. If you take too long deciding, then someone else could beat you to it. It is also possible that your application will be rejected, though if this is the case, don't despair, as there are many reasons why applications are rejected. You may have been turned down because someone else was even more suitable. The main priority for the re-homing centre is that the dog finds a home for the rest of his life where everybody gains from the relationship. If the re-homing centre believes that you are unsuitable to own a particular dog, they will let you know and give you their reasons.

GETTING TO KNOW YOUR FUTURE DOG

The next stage is to become acquainted with your new dog and introduce him to the rest of the family. If the dog has a nervous disposition or any behaviour concerns, you may be advised to visit him several times before he is ready for you to take him home. Whenever you visit him, wait for him to approach you rather than vice versa. You might know you are going to love him, but he doesn't, so let him dictate the speed at which your friendship develops. For a very nervous dog it may take more than three or four visits over several weeks.

The re-homing centre may recommend you talk to one of the behaviour advisers to ensure you know more about your new dog and the best way to handle him.

If you have children it is very important that they are confident with the new dog, and that he is not afraid of them. Even a dog with a history of successfully living in a home with children may need a careful and gradual introduction to your own; it may take time for your dog to build a relationship with each member of the family, old or young.

Although it may seem ridiculously obvious, you should also check that anyone else who lives with you – for example, grannies or lodgers – will be happy with your decision to re-home this particular dog. Many dogs are returned to re-homing centres because others in the household did not get on with them.

The Home Visit

Once you have requested to re-home a particular dog, most re-homing centres will perform a home check to verify the information you have given. During the home visit the home checker will ensure your home circumstances are suitable for the dog in question. They will often check your garden to make sure that it is securely fenced. They may also ask to see all the family, including children. Some re-homing centres may bring the dog with them to observe his interaction with you, your family and the other pets in your home.

Home visits can last from thirty minutes to an hour or two. This is also an opportunity to discuss questions or concerns you have thought of since you left. For example, will the rescue organization provide support and after-care? Will they take the dog back if things do not work out? Will they offer advice on training and behaviour, or point you in the direction of those who can? Do they have any leaflets with tips on how to settle the dog into its new home?

Going Home

When it is time to take your dog home, have everything prepared and ensure that you take things slowly. It is advisable that the day you take him home is not the day to take him on some marathon exploration trip. He will need time to settle and get to know where he is before you ask too much of him. This is an exciting day for everybody, but to ensure it is a success, care needs to be taken to move at your new dog's pace. Don't try to fit in everything you have always dreamed of doing with a dog during this crucial initial period.

'He's not what I had in mind, but I feel he's the dog for me.' Many people come across dogs that don't fit the model of their ideal dog, and it is important to assess the situation very carefully.

3 CANINE REQUIREMENTS

Every animal has a set of core needs or foundation behaviours that must be fulfilled in order for it to survive. There are also needs specific to a species, and these vary depending on the individual member. A large proportion of a dog's behaviour is driven by instinct and his 'genetic programming'; however, learning through experience also has a major influence on the way a dog behaves. It is important that owners are aware not only of the core needs of their dogs, but also those specific to the individual. Lack of awareness about behaviour requirements can result in misunderstandings, behaviour concerns and disharmony between owners and their dogs.

CORE AND INDIVIDUAL NEEDS

Core behaviour needs are concerned with the survival of the species and include drinking, feeding, urination, defecation and sleep. If we, as humans, are unable to meet any of these, we will initially

Adding extra components to your dog's environment not only adds to their enjoyment of life but also stretches them mentally.

become stressed and anxious, but if we continue to be denied the fulfilment of these needs, we will be unable to survive. Dogs as well as humans can survive if only the basic needs are met.

However, to lead a full and happy life, higher order needs must also be fulfilled. Such needs are specific to a species, and also to individuals within that species. Although a Jack Russell terrier and a border collie have the core requirements specific to any dog, other genetic influences cause one to dig holes and the other to herd sheep. In other words, it is not sufficient merely to cater for the core needs, but you must also look after the individual needs of your dog.

Engaging a Dog's Natural Abilities

We can help our dogs to become happy and healthy by providing them with opportunities to engage in their natural behaviour and abilities. Over the centuries we have selected various characteristics in dogs that are useful to us, and until fairly recent times dogs had an important role in our lives as workers rather than companions. The border collie was bred to herd sheep, and the komondor to guard them; pointers and hounds were bred for the hunt, the Siberian husky for transport, and the Jack Russell terrier to keep the rat population under control. Therefore the genes that make up these breeds affect their behaviour, and certain environmental cues can trigger them. For example, children running about will trigger the herding instinct in German shepherds and collies, while freshly dug earth will cue the digging instinct in terriers.

A dog that has never been required to do the job for which he was bred will still feel driven to do it, and will be very excited by the environmental triggers.

Harnessing these abilities and drives can give a dog an outlet for his natural programming, and in addition will help him to relax and focus when necessary.

A dog that is not sufficiently mentally or physically stimulated can become frustrated or bored, and may get up to mischief by chewing or tearing up his environment, or by disturbing the neighbours with incessant barking or howling. Part of the solution to such behaviour is increased mental and physical exercise, as a 'fully exercised' dog is less likely to engage in such activities.

Giles has become bored and frustrated, and the outlet for this is chewing the gate. In such a case give the dog a favourite ball to chew on to take his focus away from the gate, and if this behaviour becomes frequent, ask why he feels the need to act like this, and what may be missing from his life.

ROUTINE

A consistent daily routine is important to your dog, especially in the early days when he is settling in: therefore structure meal times so he can predict when food is coming and to help with house training, show him his 'safe' bed area where he can sleep and be left in peace, and set an exercise routine to keep boredom at bay. Having a daily routine is also an effective way to build your dog's confidence, as it removes uncertainty and so helps him to feel safe and secure.

To be truly contented every dog needs an outlet for his genetic potential. However, dogs are individuals and some are quite happy to sleep most of the day. Nevertheless, playing together is good for exercise and bonding between owners and their dogs. Games that develop a dog's special abilities such as herding, retrieving and hunting are especially worthwhile.

Work and Play

Dogs investigate their environment to familiarize themselves with it and to ensure that it is safe; it is one of the most prominent types of behaviour seen in all dogs, although some possess it to a higher degree. Such a dog will trot around, investigating objects with his nose and eyes, and stopping to listen to every sound. Nose work occupies and stimulates dogs naturally: it requires a lot of concentration and is an excellent way to exercise your dog mentally. Interestingly, mental exercise not only helps your dog to focus, but can be as tiring as physical activity. To engage your dog in nose work you can play 'Hide and seek' and 'Treasure trove' or some of the other games you can find in Chapters 10 and 13.

Base your play on the jobs for which your dog was bred; herding dogs such as border collies can practise their skills on giant blow-up balls, while labradors love retrieving toys.

Exercise

Walking is an integral part of the dog's genetic makeup. They share genes with wolves, whose territory may cover 20–120 square miles; the wolf pack covers roughly nine per cent of its territory per day in its search for food. Walking is very

In all weathers, dogs enjoy going out for walks and gain a great deal from mental and physical exercise.

important for the domestic dog, which is likely to become unhealthy or develop potential behaviour concerns without it. Inactive dogs can become overweight, and this in turn can stress joints, ligaments and tendons. Sending your dog out to the garden, no matter how large this is, is no substitute for a walk. This is because dogs are allelomimetic (have a tendency to copy other dogs), which means that they are more likely to wander about rather than walk briskly if left to their own devices. So you really need to be walking with your dog, each encouraging the other to 'keep up'!

The amount of exercise needed depends on your dog's age, breed and health. Generally speaking most dogs need at least thirty to sixty minutes of exercise a day, and breaking the exercise into two walks can be better than one from both a physical and psychological perspective.

The mouth and front legs must be strong as they are used to explore and interact with the environment; if dogs do not get enough exercise, they may use these parts for chewing or digging holes[8].

Tugging is instinctive for dogs, as it is a cooperative act in feeding. It also engages the mouth and front legs, which is why dogs enjoy playing 'tug of war'. However, it is not advisable to play such games with a rescue dog you know nothing about, especially if it is very nervous or fearful, or is reluctant to do so. Young children should never play this game as it is all too easy for the dog inadvertently to catch a finger in his enthusiasm.

A DOG'S SOCIAL NEEDS

Dogs are highly social animals and have evolved as such using this sociability to be cooperative not only with members of their own species but also with others; fortunately this includes humans. The need for social interaction is present in the domestic dog, and if this is missing the dog can show signs of concern.

If you have a busy lifestyle you must consider how much time you are able to spend with your dog, because to leave him alone all day, especially in a confined place lacking stimulation, can be a welfare concern in itself. If a dog is stressed and anxious when you are away he may show this by tearing up furniture, urinating or defecating, but more likely by incessant barking. Dogs are also et-epimeletic, meaning they are attention-

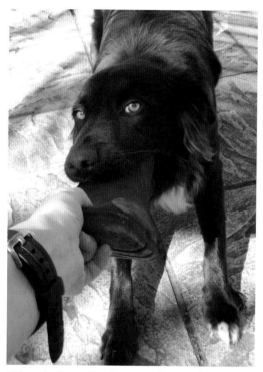

Giles playing a 'fun' game of 'tug of war'. Giles arrived with his family as a nine-week-old rescue puppy so he was able to learn these games without being concerned or threatened. This may not be the case with your new rescue dog, however, so be careful until you know him better.

and care-seeking. This behaviour is carried over from early infancy, and can be seen between adult dogs as well as between dogs and their owners.

Signs of care-seeking behaviour are whining, yelping, licking the face or hands of a person, or touching them with the paws. These behaviours can become more prominent in the dog that has an insecure attachment with his owner; furthermore he can become increasingly insecure if he is left alone for excessive periods of time.

In the photograph Thelma is jumping up and touching her handler's jacket. Although it may be tempting to push her down or turn away from her, this may only increase her insecurity as well as the intensity and frequency of this behaviour. Shaping this behaviour by asking her ask to sit and remain with all four feet on the floor, and praising her when she does so, ensures she is positively reinforced for the desired action, and this method does not involve punishment or negative reinforcement.

These two lurcher dogs came to the re-homing centre with socializing concerns, but they became great friends and periods of off-lead play together helped them overcome their issues.

Thelma is jumping up and touching her handler's jacket. Although it may be tempting to push her down or turn away from her, this may only increase her insecurity as well as the frequency of this behaviour.

If you know you need to spend time away from home on a regular basis, then you should consider re-homing a dog that will be less anxious about the situation, such as a more mature individual. (For more on attachment, refer to Chapter 11.) It is possible that an older dog, or one that is acclimatized to being left for periods of time, may be more suitable for your situation. You should discuss this with the re-homing centre so they can try to find you the right dog, but it is important to be honest.

Emotional Needs

Many owners and trainers have great faith in homoeopathic remedies for emotional concerns. Lavender oil dabbed on the inside of a dog's collar and/or some drops on their bedding has been known to have a calming effect on many dogs. It is claimed that positive results are usually seen within two to three weeks of administering Bach™ flower remedies, which can be added to food or drinking water. Although these products are natural and should be suitable for all dogs, you should consult your vet before using them.

Another interesting remedy now launched in the UK is the 'dog appeasing pheromone' (DAP™) diffuser. All lactating female mammals release an 'appeasing' pheromone, which provides a feeling of comfort, safety and reassurance to the young. Preliminary tests using a synthetic version of this indicate that DAP™ is also useful for reducing some stress in dogs[9].

Companionship can also be an effective way of helping a dog that has concerns about being left alone. If your original dog is sociable with other dogs and you have sufficient time, you could consider another canine companion.

Another alternative is to adopt two dogs at the same time, as quite often there are friendship pairs in the re-homing centre. If you have concerns about your existing dog's behaviour, then the allelomimetic (need to imitate others in the species) nature of the dog means that your new dog could well mimic the undesirable behaviour. This is an important factor to take into consideration, and if your dog is consistently suffering stress and anxiety it may be time to seek the advice of your vet and a behaviourist.

HYGIENE AND HEALTH

If you are squeamish about giving your dog a tablet, conceal it in a hot dog! We've never known it to fail. But check with your vet first, as some medications should not be given with food.

Ears

In a healthy dog the skin inside the ear should be light pink. Check his ears regularly for a deepening of this colour, as this could mean his ears are inflamed or infected. Infection can also result in a discharge, which may be yellow, dark brown, green or black, and will smell unpleasant. Another indication of ear problems is if he starts to scratch his ears or shake his head; he may also find it painful when you touch his ears.

Do not try to treat your dog yourself, and resist the temptation to clean them out with a cotton wool bud, as this can cause damage.

Eyes

Dogs with flat noses, such as pugs, boxers, bulldogs, Pekingese and so on, are more susceptible to eye problems such as redness, irritation, cloudiness, swelling and excessive weeping. If you notice any of these or other changes you

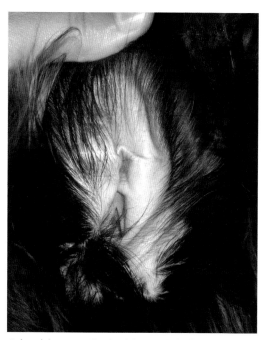

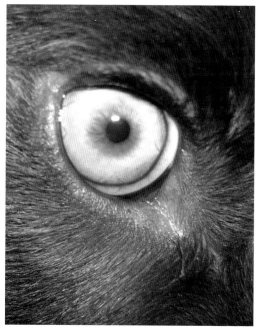

A healthy ear. The inside ear is light pink, and there is no discharge or swelling.

A healthy eye: bright and shiny, the whites indeed white and not yellow, and the lining of the eyelids pink. Do not be concerned about a small amount of mucus or occasionally watery tears, nor the third eyelid which you might see at the inside corner of the eye.

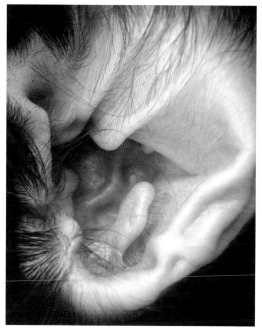

The inside of the ear is clearly visible; it appears healthy and clean.

must contact your vet.

Resist the temptation to remove foreign bodies yourself, as this could lead to permanent eye damage.

Fleas

It is unfortunate, but fleas are attracted to dogs and you can't afford to forget about them. Flea eggs lie dormant in the garden, in your carpet and in your furniture, and if left undisturbed can survive without food for about 100 days. When a suitable host passes by they use their incredible ability to jump on to it.

Apart from being unpleasant, fleas are the most common cause of skin disease in dogs, causing weeping sores, scaly skin and a strong smell. Signs that your dog may have fleas are scratching, small black specks of grit in his coat (actually this is digested dried blood), and you may even be able to see them on his skin.

When it comes to fleas, prevention is certainly better than cure. Fleas are present all year round, thriving in summer heat and in the centrally heated house. Dormant fleas can be aroused and any eggs got rid of by vacuuming the carpets two to three times a week, paying particular attention to the areas around the skirting boards. The dog's blankets should also be washed every week in the washing machine, and if possible dried in the sun. Finally, spray everywhere with an adult flea killer.

Many people use flea collars to control fleas on their dog but these may not be totally effective. An extremely effective alternative is to apply one of the spot treatments; these can only be obtained

The chair, the carpet and even the footstool are all potential breeding grounds for fleas, and Giles a potential 'host' for their next meal. Ensure your dog is up to date with his flea medication, otherwise your house and family could also suffer the consequences.

on prescription from a vet, and they work by interrupting the breeding cycle by making the females sterile.

Worms

Another unwelcome visitor is the intestinal worm. Infestation is common and can lead to ill health. Early worm detection is important because each type of dog worm requires a different form of treatment, and some of these worms can be transmitted to humans. As not all varieties of worm are visible to the naked eye, it is essential that you are aware of the symptoms. The following symptoms are typical indicators of worm infestation – although you should be aware that they may also indicate a more serious problem: dull coat, loss of weight and or appetite, a bulging stomach, coughing, loss of energy, diarrhoea and vomiting.

Resist the urge to diagnose your dog yourself, and take him to the vet who will be able to advise you on regular treatments. Control against fleas and lice is an important preventative measure as these can be hosts for tapeworms; also hygiene control is vital. Earth is better avoided for your dog's run, as this can harbour worm eggs; a surface that can be hosed down is preferable, though if this is too expensive, gravel is a reasonable alternative. Long grass can also conceal eggs, so keep your lawn short and remove dog faeces from your garden every day. Finally, make sure that you thoroughly cook any meat your dog will eat, and keep opened tins covered and in the fridge.

Calling the Vet

People often worry about the expense of taking their dog to the vet, but you have a moral obligation to do so as your dog is totally dependent on you for his wellbeing and very survival. If you take your dog to the vet at the first sign of a problem, then you are actually more likely to save yourself the expense of an operation or prolonged treatment by nipping the problem in the bud.

Signs that you might be tempted to ignore are sudden weight gain or loss or changes in temperament, as it is very easy to deceive yourself that the change is imaginary. Similarly, check out any lumps or bumps you find, as these can be the sign of a bite or something even more sinister.

Loss of appetite can be serious if it has lasted more than twenty-four hours, particularly if it is accompanied by listlessness, and the same applies to diarrhoea. Bad breath and yellow teeth are not emergencies but can lead to other problems, so should be attended to sooner rather than later. Sweet-smelling breath indicates other issues, while pale gums can represent a more serious problem.

Finally, if your dog has been in a fight, you might think there is no need to take action if he has not been seriously injured, but bites, particularly from wild animals, can cause infections. It is always best to get your dog checked by the vet if you are at all concerned that there may be a problem.

4 THE ELDERLY DOG

Although it is unwise to re-home a dog for emotional reasons exclusively, those of you with a big heart might be tempted to adopt a dog whose only shortcoming is old age. The chances are that you would be giving him the opportunity to experience contentment in this later stage of his life, and you may just be getting the dog of a lifetime.

Other advantages are that older dogs are usually calmer and gentler with children and older people, as long as they have been adequately socialized. They have also generally outgrown that poten-tially awkward chewing stage, they can be left alone for longer periods of time, and in most cases do not need constant supervision.

On the other hand the elderly dog has specific needs and potential age-related health issues, so you need to enter into this relationship fully aware of the possible problems.

The general definition of old age is the last third of the normal life expectancy for any particular breed. Larger breeds tend to age more rapidly than smaller dogs, so a Great Dane cross will be more

The old and the young both have a great deal to offer. The more mature dog may be calmer, and gentler with people.

THE LADIES AND GENTLEMEN OF THE DOG WORLD

While working at a re-homing centre Vanessa encountered her first retired sheepdog. She arrived in a van full of other dogs, some barking, some scratching to come out, yet others frozen and fearful. This dog, on the other hand, was sitting calmly in her crate, patiently waiting for someone to come and see her. When Vanessa put on her lead, she looked up, waiting for the next command. This nine-year-old border collie had entered the rescue environment because of a change of situation and she was no longer able to work. Fortunately her farmer owner very much wanted to find her a retirement home, and so here she was. The next day many visitors showed an interest in her, and within two weeks she was taken home by a family who were absolutely thrilled to find her.

This was not an isolated event, as month after month beautiful older dogs would quickly enter and then leave the re-homing centre, some retired from a working background, others sadly homeless through the loss of their owners. Although some older dogs have concerns much as their youthful counterparts, most of these dogs are truly the ladies and gentlemen of the dog world.

mature at five years old than his small terrier kennelmate of the same age. This is not a hard and fast rule, however, because if a dog, whether large or small, has a genetic predisposition to a specific disease this may also affect his lifespan.

COMMON SIGNS OF AGEING

Whether or not you are specifically looking for an older dog, it is useful to recognize the physical changes that signify maturity. Many senior dogs begin to accumulate grey hairs, particularly around the muzzle area. The coat sometimes becomes a little sparser and coarser in texture, and the eyes may be blue and opaque because of cataracts.

More mature dogs can be a little more 'laid back' and less active, but this varies according to the individual. Not all dogs age at the same rate; some dogs turn prematurely grey, just like humans, and this can be due to stress. It is not unknown for middle-aged dogs with relatively dark muzzles to arrive at re-homing centres and within a year become very grey.

Ageing, and the changes in behaviour

Some middle-aged dogs become prematurely grey, so always check a dog's age before assuming he is either old or young. Champ looks much older than he actually is, and those who think he is a laid back elderly dog would be greatly mistaken.

that accompany it, can be influenced by environmental factors, so by providing a suitable environment you can increase the possibility that your dog will reach his genetic potential for maximum lifespan.

PROVIDING A STRESS-FREE ENVIRONMENT

What is most needed when preparing for ownership of the elderly dog is a large dose of common sense. Both humans and dogs are less able to cope with stress as they age, so the first priority is to aim for a stress-free environment. There is more about a dog's view of stress in Chapter 10, but the following contingencies should be considered.

Make sure that your dog's bed is in a warm, quiet, draught-free place where he will not be disturbed by people constantly walking past, or be pestered by children or other pets. Dogs of all ages need to be able to relieve themselves easily, but the elderly dog may be slower in both recognizing the need and in getting to the place where he can relieve himself. Bear this in mind in your planning.

Elderly dogs often have poor sight and hearing, so place the bed against a wall so he can see all around and has no need to monitor the space behind him.

It is important that your dog can get out of his bed easily and that his weight is distributed evenly to reduce pressure on his joints.

Hypothermia and severe pain from arthritis can occur in the winter. Make sure he has a blanket on his bed in cold weather, and if he is reluctant to go out

Buster can relax as he is in his own corner, well out of everyone's way. He is so content that he has taken to sleeping upside down with his legs in the air, a clear sign that he is at ease with his environment.

in cold weather provide him with a 'coat' to keep his joints warm.

In the summer elderly dogs can suffer from heatstroke and bloat. Some of the signs of heatstroke are excessive panting, increased salivation, and dry gums that become pale, greyish and tacky. Prevention being better than cure. It is important to ensure your dog can lie out of direct sunlight and has access to shade and water. A coat clip may help some breeds to cope with the heat.

It is advisable to keep a close eye on older dogs when they are outside during hot weather as some quite literally forget to seek shade. Some dogs simply love sun bathing. It is advisable to supervise and even limit the time they spend outside when temperatures are high. Additionally, limiting walks to early mornings and evenings when the sun is low is a useful management technique during summer months. This can help to protect the older dog from the possible harmful effects associated with warmer weather.

As mentioned, bloat is one such concern (abnormal build-up of air/fluid in the stomach); larger dogs and those with deep or narrow chests can be more prone. Causes such as stress, swallowing air and fluids when drinking while panting heavily can be rife in summer, so taking extra care to monitor and keep the elderly dog cool and protected is certainly beneficial. It is definitely important to take him to the vet, as the problem could become serious.

Arthritis is a common problem, but even if your dog is just stiff and sore, provide a ramp for him to get up and down from higher areas such as your car or furniture. Larger dogs can be helped by raising their food and water bowls: raised feeders make eating and drinking more comfortable if there is stiffness in the neck or back.

Deterioration of the brain can be lessened by providing a stimulating environment; for example, hiding the dog's food around the garden keeps both his mind and his body active. New toys and games will arouse his curiosity. We know that a reduction of oxygen to the brain results in impaired brain function, so encourage more oxygen to circulate by gentle exercise. Once again, monitor your dog's reaction to any games you play with him, and avoid them if he becomes frustrated or confused.

Reduce stress by anticipating stressful events. For example, watch his reaction to potentially stressful influences, such as other dogs or children, and move him to a safe distance if he becomes anxious. As you come to know your dog better, you will become aware of who or what causes him to feel particularly stressed.

Dogs feel secure when their environment is predictable, and they know what is expected of them. A major source of stress is any change in routine, so the number one priority is to firmly and quickly establish a routine.

CARE OF THE OLDER DOG

Caring properly for an elderly dog is all about prevention, as some illnesses become more likely with age. Early detection of disease is vital if the dog is to have the best chance of coping, so regular vet checks are crucial. You must also consult your vet about keeping your dog up to date on all vaccinations carried out by the re-homing centre.

It is also important to keep a lookout for any changes, as these could be a sign of more serious illness: for example an increase in urination, appetite and thirst can be signs of diabetes, while tiring more quickly and excessive panting or coughing may indicate cardio-pulmonary problems. The golden rule is: if in doubt, call the vet.

Diet

The older dog may have a weaker sense of smell and taste, and the digestive organs may become less efficient in digesting and absorbing food. Therefore he may need to be fed a tasty, highly digestible diet. Food which is specially formulated for elderly dogs will strengthen your dog's immune system, and as they contain fewer calories, should control his weight.

In order to prevent urinary diseases, make sure your dog has a balanced diet containing high levels of protein and phosphorus, although these may need to be decreased if he has kidney problems.

If your dog behaves as though he is still hungry, try distracting him before you give him more food; involve him in some simple training or games, as he may be carrying out ritualized behaviour patterns, and this will help him to use his brain constructively.

Common Physical Malfunctions

Gum Disease

Regular dental care is important throughout a dog's life, but it becomes crucial as he enters his later years. Disease of the gums and plaque-encrusted teeth are both painful conditions and can lead to loss of teeth, which obviously affects his ability to chew and therefore his digestion. If bacteria enter the bloodstream through inflamed gums, secondary infections can occur in the kidney, liver or heart valves.

It is possible to prevent this by regularly checking your dog's gums for inflammation and abnormal colour. If the gums don't look healthy, see your vet right away. Brush your dog's teeth regularly with a dog toothbrush, give hard food instead of soft canned food, and give him toys to chew, all of which will help to remove plaque from his teeth. If your dog's breath is at all smelly, he may have gum disease or have had an adverse reaction to his food. The first thing you will need to do is take him to the vet for a check-up.

Heart Disease

Older pets are more susceptible to diseases of the heart and lungs. Signs of heart disease include coughing, wheezing and breathing difficulties, or weakness and sometimes fainting. If you notice any of these signs, contact your vet quickly because if the condition is dealt with in the early stages, medication can enable your dog to lead a long and normal life.

Skin Disorders

As dogs age their skin may become dry and irritated or thinner and less elastic, making it more vulnerable to tearing and injury. A dull, thinning coat is a feature of ageing, but equally it may be a sign of disease or nutritional deficiency, so should be checked by a vet. If your vet decides that there are no health reasons for the coat changes, he will be able to recommend a suitable supplement or change in diet.

Regular grooming increases coat and skin health, and has the additional advantage of making it more likely that changes in coat and skin condition will be noticed.

Urinary Incontinence

An elderly dog that has been house trained for years may suddenly start to urinate in inappropriate places. This can be caused by problems with the part of the nervous system that controls the bladder, or by disorders of the urinary tract, prostate, or other body systems.

Frequent urination, foul-smelling urine, blood in the urine, or no urination at all are common signs of dog urinary tract infections. Other signs might be drinking unusually large amounts of water or constantly licking the genitals. Spotting the symptoms and treating them early may make the difference between life and death for your dog.

Arthritis

Stiffness, limping, or favouring a limb are all common signs of arthritis, particularly after sleep or resting. Your dog may also be reluctant to jump or even to climb stairs, and in some cases might not be able to get on his feet without help.

Dog arthritis, or osteoarthritis, is a degenerative disease and may be worse in cold, damp weather; it is also more likely if there has been previous damage to the joint or if the dog is overweight. Arthritis is a progressive condition that involves the breakdown of cartilage and inflammation of a joint, causing pain and swelling.

Although there is no cure, you can make sure that your arthritic dog is

Exercise is important for the elderly dog, and many enjoy their walks just as much as they did when they were younger.

comfortable in his everyday life. Dogs with arthritis should still be exercised, but not excessively, as that can make their arthritis worse: gentle walks and swimming help maintain muscle mass, which reduces stress on joints. Once again your dog must see the vet to ensure the correct diagnosis is made.

Weight Problems

Being either overweight or underweight can be a problem in older dogs. Elderly dogs tend to have a slower metabolism and gain weight rapidly, which puts a strain on the heart and stress on joints. Inadequate exercise, and feeding an elderly dog the same amount as a more active dog, are the main causes of obesity. If he is overweight, it may be advisable to put him on a low calorie diet (under veterinary supervision), and definitely choose treats that are low in fat and sugar.

Offering your elderly dog opportunities to do physical and mental 'work' is therefore important in his daily routine. It is, however, important to take care that he doesn't 'overdo it'.

If your dog doesn't use his muscles he will lose mass and tone, and it will become harder for him to move about. Under veterinary supervision short but

This elderly spaniel is enjoying a rest. His coat is a little sparse in places. It is important to monitor the elderly dog and note any physical and psychological changes.

frequent walks or swims will not only help to control his weight, but will also keep him in shape.

THE AGEING PROCESS OF THE BRAIN

In a youthful dog, the brain sends messages from cell to cell through connecting filaments. In the ageing dog, the filaments contract and lose some of their contacts with other cells. This means that information must pass through a different route. This slows the speed of information processing from 225mph at peak fitness to about 50mph.

Another problem is that once stimulated, the cells remain programmed for abnormally long periods, preventing further information from being absorbed. This affects a dog's short-term memory, making him irritable when disturbed, slow to obey commands, and causing problems with orientation and learning. Previous daily activities became ritualized so that he may, for example, ask to be let out to urinate not because of need but because some cue has stimulated the cell linked to this action. The cell cannot begin to evaluate the cue; it merely triggers imprinted actions. The dog may also, for example, return to his food bowl for a second helping because the original cue remains and he is unable to override the imprinted actions. This may lead to him merely nibbling at the 'second helping', or in severe cases wolfing the whole lot down.

However, all is not lost because both humans and dogs can prevent the ageing processes of the brain by applying the adage: 'Use it or lose it.' This means you must continue to stimulate your dog with an interesting environment with plenty of toys and games.

Sensory Losses

As a dog ages, changes occur to the sensory system that feeds information into the dog's brain. Food loses flavour, high notes cannot be heard, and the loss of hair cells in the ears can lead to deafness. You will know that your dog's hearing is failing when he doesn't respond to your verbal commands. Ear infections can also lead to poor hearing. Signs of ear infections include discharge from the ear, persistent head shaking, or pawing the ear.

A dog uses hearing as part of his danger detection system, and failure to detect threats in the form of other dogs or people can be very disturbing. This means you must ensure that other dogs or people do not take him by surprise. In addition it can be very beneficial to both you and your dog to teach him hand signals to replace and assist your vocal commands.

Failing eyesight creates similar problems. With age comes the loss of both types of retinal cell in the eyes, and the lenses lose their elasticity so the dog is unable to focus properly and vision is blurred.

A possible sign that your dog's eyesight is deteriorating is misjudging spaces or walking into objects. To make life less stressful for your dog, you should talk to him as he approaches you, and try to keep everything in the same position. If you have to move familiar things, then make sure you have shown your dog around so he is aware of the changes.

5 RESCUE PUPPIES

If you are considering a puppy from a re-homing centre you may not have a great deal of information on his background. This is especially true if he was found as a stray. It is therefore essential to be aware of the stages of development so you do not interpret a normal developmental change as something more sinister.

THE FIRST STAGE OF DEVELOPMENT

From twenty-one to 112 days the puppy's brain is far more impressionable (neuro-scientists use the term 'plastic') than in maturity. This plasticity has both a positive and a negative side: on the positive side, it means that a puppy's brain is more open to learning and enriching influences. On the negative side, it means he is just as likely to learn undesirable behaviour as the behaviours you want him to learn.

This means that behaviours which are sweet and endearing in a puppy may be totally undesirable in an older dog. For example, when your puppy begs at meal-times it is essential that you resist those doe eyes and keep your food for yourself, because if you feed him from your plate now, he will expect to receive food from you every time you eat, and when you have a fully grown adult dog salivating over your dinner plate you will rue the day you gave in. The message is clear: do not feed your dog from your plate what-ever age he is, because if you do, and then later you tell him not to, you will confuse him because you are then being inconsistent. Begging is not naughty behaviour; you have simply trained him to do it!

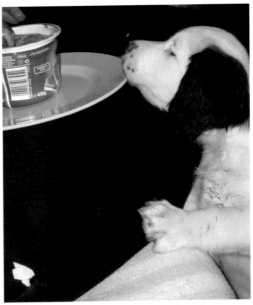

This young puppy is investigating the source of a very appealing smell, but you must resist those doe eyes and keep your food for yourself because if you feed him from your plate now, he will expect you to do so every time you eat.

A puppy's first set of teeth are very sharp, and puppy bites can be very painful. However, a set of mature teeth can do much more damage.

Puppies are very adaptable, and also sensitive to everyday life experiences. Everything is new to them, and it is very important that these early experiences are positive.

Another such behaviour is 'mouthing', when a puppy will wrap his mouth around your arm or your hand. This is what they do when playing with other puppies, and while we may not object to this when he is twelve weeks old, a two-year-old German shepherd doing the same thing is another matter altogether.

It is essential that the whole household has decided on target behaviour and associated commands when the puppy arrives home. You all must be absolutely consistent in your behaviour towards him, otherwise you will confuse him and it is unlikely he will learn effectively. An important role in the training of desirable behaviour is played by positive reinforcement, where something good happens when the dog behaves in a specific way. It is so much easier to achieve training goals through rewarding your puppy for doing what you would like him to do, rather than punishing him for doing something you find undesirable. Punishment has no place in training, and such an approach can be very damaging to your puppy's attachment status – the relationship he has with you.

The use of training techniques will be explained in more detail in Chapter 13, however it is critically important to take the time to 'shape' your puppy's behaviour from the first day you have him, to encourage the development of a well adjusted adult.

THE SECOND STAGE OF DEVELOPMENT

On the forty-ninth day the brain of the puppy is the same as that of a mature dog, and he is emotionally developed and ready to learn. This is an advantageous age to re-home a puppy, as his brain is like a new computer ready to be programmed, and like a computer he will learn quickly and remember what he has learnt.

For the next five weeks you should give your puppy a wide variety of experiences and teach him the commands your family has agreed upon. However, training sessions of more than fifteen minutes can be self-defeating, as a puppy has a short attention span and can get tired very quickly. It is preferable to keep them short and fun. Any new experience should be introduced in a calm way so that your puppy does not feel threatened. Human babies need a safe base from which they can explore the world, and so do puppies. The safe base for a human baby is his parent; for your puppy the attachment figure is you or a member of your household.

HABITUATION TO THE BIG WIDE WORLD

There is a great deal for a puppy to learn when you first bring him into his new home. It is essential to expose him to the 'wide world', and introduce him to the many scenarios he will face. This is achieved by the process of habituation, which means becoming accustomed to key items in his environment and learning that there is no need to be concerned.

This is particularly important during what is known as the 'fear imprint period', which occurs from eight to eleven weeks. This is a time when the dog's ancestors would have learned to avoid real threats in his environment, such as natural predators, and to a lesser extent harmful plants and places. The domestic dog is surrounded by potential threats to his safety, and could develop a long-lasting fear during this period.

Therefore you must ensure he is not startled when you switch on any of your appliances, from hair dryers to washing machines.

It is also important that he develops confidence with all people, including children and visitors (so make sure he can, by supervising introductions and any rough play!). At this point introduce him to the car, and get him accustomed to short journeys and visits to the vet.

It is important to do all this with care, and to expose your puppy to new sights and sounds gradually; if he becomes fearful, then take a step back and build up his confidence again from a less threatening stimulus. For instance, do not start introducing him to traffic on a main road, because this is likely to 'flood' his senses – to overwhelm him – and may lead to a fear response that will be activated when similar events occur in the future.

Instead, take him to a quiet location with plenty of space to move away if he seems concerned, and acclimatize him gently to the many sights and sounds of the world. Many puppies benefit from wearing a harness when out on walks because it takes the pressure off their necks as they learn to walk on the lead.

EARLY SOCIALIZATION

It is also important that your puppy becomes 'socialized', which means learning to recognize and interact with the humans and other animals he is likely to meet, including his own species. Socialization is very important, as a puppy without this background knowledge and foundation training can become an adult predisposed to be fearful or defensive in such encounters.

Socializing with a variety of dogs is the best way for a puppy to learn how to

This puppy is participating in a socializing session with two older dogs. This early socialization must be maintained and developed so he grows into a well-adjusted adult capable of meeting strange dogs without fear.

interact with members of his own species, and for general games and fun. Dogs begin life with their fellow littermates and are therefore sociable from birth, but this early socialization must be maintained and developed: even when you have successfully socialized your puppy to humans, dogs and other animals in his life, and he is habituated to potential threats, you cannot relax your efforts, for two reasons. First, research has shown that socialization and habituation can wear off; and secondly, adolescence appears to affect dogs as much as it does humans, and any progress made up to this point seems to be overturned! This means you must continually reinforce socialization and habituation up to maturity at about four years.

ADOLESCENCE

The onset and length of adolescence varies according to breed, although the average is from nine to eighteen months. Smaller breeds are generally through the adolescent period by the time they are a year old; larger breeds may take up to an additional year to reach maturity. To further cloud the issue, there are individual differences within breeds.

There are some dogs who are relatively immature whose behaviour is similar to a puppy's right into mature adulthood. This factor can be very much down to personality. Many labrador cross-bred dogs fit this description and can make the most wonderful companions.

As the dog reaches adolescence his hormones are preparing him for life as an adult. As a result he instinctively begins to make decisions for himself in preparation for the time when he will leave his family and go off into the world to start one of his own.

What happens to the domestic dog at this age is totally confusing for him. He is ready to make his own decisions and he is training himself to be independent, but he is faced with a situation that is contrary to all his programming. We continue to mother him, provide him with food and shelter, and boss him about. What is he to do? In fact, he does what his body tells him to do: he prepares for an independent life and starts to think for himself.

Training schools get most of their calls from owners of dogs of this age, and the peak age for rescue dogs is between nine and eighteen months. Although many of these dogs are likely to make a bad impression on potential owners, they could make fantastic companions. What they need is careful, kind, considered and sympathetic handling.

Handling the Adolescent

What alarms most new dog owners is the perceived change in their puppy's behaviour at this time. He may ignore well-learned commands, he may no longer come when called, or he may wander away when off his lead. It is common for owners to believe that they have been misled into buying a difficult dog, or that he is being defiant or establishing dominance.

There is a physiological change which affects cognition, but the resulting behaviour must not be ascribed human motives: he is not testing you – he is a dog, not an undergraduate; he is not entering a leadership battle – he is a dog, not a politician; and he is not defying you – he is a dog, not a wayward pupil.

Your puppy has become an adolescent, and needs a secure, controlled environment in which he can learn to be a mature adult. He will require additional training and focus in his life at this point to give him an outlet for his developing mental and physical abilities.

Both dogs in this photograph are adolescents. The larger collie type dog on the left is a confident individual, unlike the spaniel lying in a very submissive position due to the collie's rough play.

The Key to Success

If you have had your puppy from a very young age you will already have a set of procedures to deal with his wandering attention. You must avoid thinking that he is being 'naughty', as this leads to frustration and anger and can be very destructive in your relationship. Regard this instead as a period of 'over-learning', so that for every command he appears to have forgotten, you return to the way you first taught him.

If you have adopted an 'adolescent' from a re-homing centre you must be very patient and train him as though he had never had any previous training.

BEHAVIOURAL AND PHYSIOLOGICAL CHANGES IN ADOLESCENCE

- The body of the intact adolescent male dog produces testosterone at several times the rate of an adult. As a result, some male-oriented behaviours can become more extreme at this stage of life. Some dogs begin to be more defensive towards other dogs, while others become protective and territorial.
- Occasional lapses or even a complete loss of attention can arise from raging hormones.
- As the puppy matures sexually, the male begins to lift his leg to urinate.
- Both genders may start to urinate indoors.
- Intact males begin to mark their territory with urine. This is often accompanied by an increase in sniffing behaviour (every tree becomes a fascination).
- Males often try to taste female urine as a way of telling whether or not the female is in season.
- The female has her first season from six to twelve months, and if not pregnant may develop false pregnancies.
- At around six to ten months the teeth set in the jaw, and the adult teeth grow in. This means the jaw is likely to be uncomfortable.
- The puppy coat is replaced by the adult coat, starting down the spine.
- The dog's behaviour may regress to that more typical of a puppy.

The adolescent male in the yellow collar is posturing in this greeting with an older male. This is shown by the high tail carriage, high head posture and raised hair over the shoulder area.

This young collie male is sniffing the hedge to find out more about the dogs who 'marked' this as their 'territory'. This behaviour becomes more frequent as your puppy grows into an adolescent.

The Golden Rules

The golden rules at this stage of his training are as follows:

- Make sure he gets something out of each training session – praise, a reward or fun.
- Present it as fun.
- Use favourite toys and treats to reward his successes.
- Be patient: getting annoyed won't help either of you.
- Keep your training sessions short – fifteen minutes maximum.

Helpful Strategies

Exercise such as walking, off-lead running, and mental workouts such as training and fun games (see Chapter 13) will help to meet your dog's mental and physical requirements. This is very important in helping to combat boredom and stress, and to help your dog to focus when required.

Taking your dog to training classes can be beneficial for several reasons. First, they give you a structure to work to, and realistic expectations. They help to socialize your dog to other dogs and to people. They provide opportunities for over-learning, which is essential for habituation and socialization. There are also many clubs and activities you can become involved in, such as agility, heelwork to music, and many more. These can be fantastic fun for owner and dog alike; such activities are also great opportunities to exercise your dog both mentally and physically, and to help meet his requirements.

Spaying or neutering dogs at a relatively young age (six to ten months) can modify some of the behaviours associated with adolescence and adulthood.

Puppy/Adolescent Concerns

Typical puppy behaviour includes using the teeth in mouthing and biting, and chewing. Mouthing or actually biting must be monitored, controlled and 'shaped' into other behaviours when possible. Chewing, on the other hand, is essential to the puppy's development. At between four and eight months the puppy loses his milk teeth and his permanent teeth start to grow, and this is uncomfortable for him and makes his urge to chew very strong. Chewing also helps to align the teeth correctly along the jawbone.

A dog's need to chew is so intense that he may chew any available object. These objects may be specific toys bought for the purpose, or they may be your personal belongings. While it is annoying to find your belongings chewed or damaged, it is worth bearing in mind that your belongings are not designed for a dog's powerful jaws, and splinters of harmful materials can easily end up in your dog's stomach, causing much distress and possibly expensive vet bills. To avoid such disasters, some common sense actions need to be taken:

- Provide a varied and plentiful supply of toys and chews.
- Keep the areas your puppy uses free of inappropriate items such as shoes, children's toys and papers.
- Make sure that your puppy is confined to a safe area where there is nothing he can chew when unsupervised.

If your puppy is chewing something inappropriate, try to get his attention without shouting at him or telling him off. If it is an object that is small and movable such as a shoe, always swap the item for something else by offering a toy or a treat instead of the object he already has. If you are unable to move the object your puppy is chewing, such as a table leg, use the same principle and offer an alternative object to chew on. Chewing is such a natural behaviour that it is important to remember that your puppy is not being naughty when he chooses your shoe over his toy.

As puppies like to chew and dismantle many house and garden items, it is important to keep dangerous objects out of his reach and ensure he has 'safe' toys to play with, which are the correct size for him even when he is supervised. Toys that are too small can be easily swallowed, which can be potentially life threatening. If you either see or suspect your puppy has eaten something potentially harmful to him, or that could cause an obstruction, it is important to take

This young puppy has decided to focus some of his chewing energy on this piece of material; unfortunately it is actually a dressing gown being worn at the time. Handle this sort of situation calmly: replacing the gown with a toy or chew is a more effective way of intervening than shouting at him.

him to the vet. Your vet may be able to induce vomiting or retrieve the object from the stomach without surgery, but the longer the time since ingestion the less likely this option becomes.

MATURITY

Between the ages of one and four years your puppy will become sexually mature (as opposed to fully grown). You must continue to train him during this period. If your young dog becomes fearful towards a stimulus at this point, take care in handling the situation. Do not force him to do anything he is reluctant to try, and tackle any concerns with consideration.

Safety First

Puppies are like children in that they want to touch and explore everything. The golden rule is therefore to move or secure anything that can break, or that could choke, poison, strangle or trap him. This includes flimsy toys, curtains, electrical wires, open cupboards, chemical cleaning materials, shelving and any other item of possible concern. Look at his environment from his viewpoint – literally: lie on the floor and see what catches your eye.

At this stage it may be wasteful to buy a top-of-the-range dog bed as he may chew and damage it. A more practical alternative is a cheaper hard bed, or even a cardboard box with one side removed and lined with some really warm and comfortable bedding; old woollen jumpers and blankets make great cosy beds. As he matures you will be able to buy him whichever bed you choose, but save this until he has at least got over the teething period.

HOMECOMING

When your puppy arrives home, ensure that everyone is very calm and gentle when handling him. Do not force yourselves on him, and give him time to explore and come to you. Speak gently and soothingly. Each person should allow him to sniff their hands and stroke him gently, but be careful not to lean over him.

Do ensure you begin house training straightaway: take your puppy to the garden when he arrives home, repeating this at least every thirty minutes while you are with him. If he begins to circle or start sniffing the floor, take him outside saying 'toilet', and wait until he relieves himself, rewarding him when he does so.

Puppies, like human babies, cannot hold themselves up for long periods of time when they need to go to the toilet. Therefore when you are not able to supervise him – such as during the night, or when you are out of the house – lay training pads or newspaper on a small area of the floor in your puppy's 'safe' area. House training is discussed in more detail in Chapter 9, but at this stage it is absolutely vital to remember not to punish your puppy for making house-training mistakes.

Eventually, once he has eaten and been taken to the toilet for the last time in the night, he will be sleepy and ready for bed. Put his bed where he will not be disturbed when you want to make a cup of tea or run upstairs. Puppies need time to sleep and process all the information they have learnt during the day, and therefore need a safe and quiet place to get their required rest. Sleep is a 'core need', and if it is jeopardized the dog's behaviour and welfare is likely to be affected.

He may also appreciate a piece of bedding from his former home, or some soft toys to snuggle up to; even a ticking alarm clock can give some comfort, as can a softly playing radio. A hot water bottle can be very comforting – though obviously this must be of the 'pet safe' variety.

Puppies need a safe and quiet place to get their required rest. Sleep is a 'core need', and if it is jeopardized, the dog's behaviour and welfare are likely to be affected.

6 PREPARING THE HOME

Your new dog may be confused, stressed or even fearful when he is first brought home. It is to be hoped that he will have had a chance to get to know you while still at the re-homing centre, but you are bringing him into a completely new environment and this is likely to be very disorienting. It will help him to settle if you have done your best to prepare your home, and this chapter aims to help you do just that.

BASIC EQUIPMENT

Collars, Leads and Extras

Collars are essential, not only for the control and safety of your dog, but for compliance with the law. The Control of Dogs Order 1992 stipulates that all dogs must wear a collar and an identity tag in a public place. The identity tag must show the name and address of the owner, and your dog must still wear an identity tag even if he is micro-chipped. If you fail to comply with this law you can be fined up to £5,000. The few dogs exempt from this rule include police dogs, guide dogs for the blind, and dogs used for help with emergency rescue work.

You need to measure your dog's neck before you buy a collar, as it needs to be slack enough to be comfortable but not so that he can slip out of it. Once you have measured his neck, add 3in (7.5cm) to give you the length of collar you must buy. Collars with a smooth finish on the inside limit rubbing or irritation, and while leather collars are long lasting, they may be too heavy for small dogs. If you can't get two fingers under the collar when it is done up, it is too small. There is a great variety of collars out there in many different sizes, colours, patterns and textures, but the most important feature is the fit!

Avoid any type of choke chain: they do what they say on the label, and choke the dog when he pulls. Such devices can cause real injury, such as rupturing the windpipe and bruising the outer and

This dog's collar is well fitting, with the identity tag clearly showing.

inner ear. They have also been known to cause epileptic fits triggered by constriction of blood supply to the brain, and neuromuscular disorders from constriction of the cervical region of the spine. There are much safer and more effective ways of training your dog to walk on the lead, therefore please invest time in these alternatives.

The main thing to consider when buying a lead is the length. Longer leads are more suitable for fully trained dogs, while leads with a maximum stretch of 3 to 4ft (1m) will give you more control over your new dog. Retractable leads, which extend at the touch of a button, give your dog freedom to roam further and will give you control even at a distance. These, however, are more suitable for dogs that are fully lead-trained, as the retractable lead's large handle can make it difficult to control dogs that pull or lunge.

The double-clip lead is ideal (with a clip on each end) because it gives owners greater flexibility: they can change the length of lead when needed, and can use it in conjunction with other items, such as a harness. Clipping one end of the lead on the collar and the other end on the harness gives greater control over the dog's head and body simultaneously. While it is still possible to have control over the head area, it also helps you to be more sympathetic to the dog's neck and body because the 'double points of contact' enable you to be aware of any tension building. These two points of contact also mean that you can change where the lead is clipped on to, depending on your dog's behaviour or where you are going: if you are close to a road the shortened lead would be useful, but while you are in a park you may wish to give him more freedom and lengthen the lead.

The two points of contact give you great flexibility because you can change where the lead is clipped on so that it is shorter or longer.

This 'rein' effect can be extremely useful, and unlike the retractable leads, this one has a handle, which is easier to hold and manoeuvre. These leads are multifunctional, and can help you in teaching the dog to walk loose on a longer lead (use the full length of lead) right through to training him to keep close by your side when near a road for example (shorten the lead).

Harnesses benefit many types of dogs, especially those who may have handling or collar concerns, as pressure is taken off the neck area and the tension distributed throughout the body, helping you to guide the dog more easily. There are many styles of harness available on the market which help to keep the dog balanced while under restraint and can alleviate pulling. You do not necessarily need an anti-pull design, a standard harness can be the most beneficial for walking and training a wide variety of dogs, especially when used in conjunction with a collar connection, at least until the dog has become accustomed to the change of pressure.

Head collars can also make a considerable difference to dogs. However, we once again advise you to use this equipment in conjunction with a harness or collar connection. The head collar has most benefit when used sympathetically as a 'tool' to guide the dog's head rather than for restraint alone. If used in conjunction with another connection you can 'guide' the head while taking some pressure off this sensitive area when you need to. If your dog begins to shake his head you are putting too much pressure on the face and he could become frustrated and concerned. By having that extra contact you can instantly alleviate the pressure and help your dog to relax and learn what you are trying to reinforce.

In the Car

At some point you are going to take your dog in the car, even if this is only from the re-homing centre to your home. This means your dog needs to be restrained to safeguard him from injury and to prevent him from distracting you while driving. While there is no specific law obliging you to restrain your dog in a car, clearly you will be liable if he causes you to have an accident.

The safest place for him is in a crate, as his movement will be restricted. If this isn't possible, obtain a dog seatbelt, which doubles as a harness. If you have an estate car, you can fit a mesh dog guard to keep him at the back. He should be kept in the back for several reasons: in the front seat he can be thrown into the windshield if you have to make a sudden stop; he can climb on the driver's lap; and if for some reason the air bags are activated, the force can severely injure a dog. When you bring him from the re-homing centre be prepared in case he gets queasy in the car: cover the seats, bring paper towels, and give him plenty of air.

Introducing New Equipment

It is very important that any new item of equipment is introduced gradually. It may take several sessions, each of just a few minutes' duration at any one time, and using positive reinforcement. Do not leave your dog unattended when wearing any equipment as he could get caught up and injure himself.

Every dog is an individual, and some dogs will not respond favourably to certain items of equipment, and behaviour concerns can be created by their use. While one dog may be quite happy with your chosen method of restraint, another may become extremely stressed and frustrated with the same method. This can even lead to redirection (being unable to assault the restraint, the dog redirects his frustration by snapping at his owner). It is therefore important to review your dog's behaviour when wearing any item of equipment, old or new. Some items may just not suit your dog, and you will not gain anything by using them.

Bowls

Your dog will need two bowls, one for food and one for water, although in the interests of hygiene it is advisable to get duplicates for when one set is in the wash. Plastic bowls are a breeding ground for germs as they are more chewable. For health reasons, use stainless steel as dogs tend not to chew them and they can be sterilized. Porcelain or earthenware bowls without painted surfaces can also be used and are heavier than steel so are less likely to be pushed around when the dog is eating. Wash both regularly and thoroughly, away from the family dishes.

Beds

The type and position of your new dog's bed is very important as his bed should be a place where he can feel safe and comfortable without being disturbed. At the end of his first day with you he will probably be feeling quite bewildered, and will appreciate a cosy 'den' where he can settle for the night.

Many dogs like to stretch out while relaxing or sleeping, and it is important they have plenty of room to do this. Larger beds can be packed with bedding to fill them out to make very comfortable

Ensure your dog has access to water day and night. Porcelain is a hygienic material for a food or water bowl. The stainless-steel food bowl has a blue rubber rim around the base to prevent it slipping when the dog eats. Both bowls are on a tray to catch any spills.

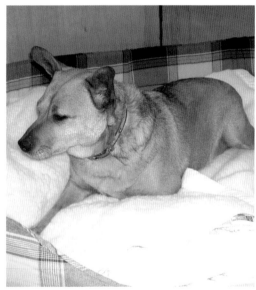

Larger beds can be packed with bedding to make them a comfortable sleeping area. Many dogs like to stretch out while relaxing or sleeping, and it is important they have plenty of room to do this.

and cosy sleeping areas. You can use old blankets or bedcovers to do this, and these are just as effective and comfortable as new purpose-made covers from a pet shop. They are also considerably less expensive.

In order to calculate the size of bed your dog needs, measure him in his normal sleeping position from the nose or front legs to the back legs, and add nine to twelve inches. Choose a bed that fits that measurement; if you choose a round bed, the diameter of the bed should be the same as this measurement. If you are unable to get a bed which is the exact size, go for the next size up: larger beds are not a problem, but chopping off some of the dog's extra length could well be!

Look for a bed that can be cleaned regularly and is raised a few inches off the floor away from draughts. However, do not buy a raised bed for a dog with orthopaedic problems, or breeds such as dachshunds which are prone to back problems. You need not go to the expense of a special pad for the bed, just line it with something soft and washable such as an old blanket or even a duvet you no longer use.

Place the bed away from areas where people frequently walk; this will ensure no one trips over it, and the dog will not be disturbed. It should also be in a warm part of the room away from draughts.

There are several reasons for and against allowing your dog to share your bed or bedroom. If your dog needs to go out, he will not then wake the whole neighbourhood in order to gain your attention. Some dogs get very lonely at night, and being near to you will comfort them. On the other hand, hygiene is a

The home environment can flood the newly re-homed rescue dog's senses, so it will help him if you place his bed in a safe and secluded position.

negative factor; also sleeping with you can make some dogs overly dependent and lead to separation concerns.

However, at the end of the day, where your dog sleeps is your choice, and will depend on the individual. It is, however, preferable not to encourage your dog to sleep on the bed, especially one you know little about; this way you can avoid conflicts arising if you decide you don't want him on your bed. So be consistent and keep him on the floor. He won't know when he has muddy paws, and unless you are quite happy with his prints all over your sheets, start as you mean to go on.

Dog Crates

If you are considering a dog crate, check with the re-homing centre if using one is suitable for the dog you are re-homing. Some dogs simply cannot cope with being confined in a crate – for example, those that become anxious when left alone. If your prospective dog has been not been acclimatized to crate use, a great deal of training will be necessary before he is ready for confinement. Crating can cause stress and anxiety for many dogs, especially those not prepared for it.

The rationale for crate use is that dogs are 'den' animals and gravitate towards den-like dwellings. However, although both the domestic dog's wild ancestors and his feral relatives may use 'den dwellings', they are free to come and go, whereas in some households the dog can be confined in a crate for eight to ten hours without a break, which can cause significant psychological problems.

If crates are introduced properly and used appropriately they can provide a safe place to leave your dog for short periods of time away from possible threats or concerns. They can also be a tool when house training your dog, as it is innate in healthy dogs not to urinate or defecate in the den or bed area.

We recommend the crate to be used in conjunction with a room or smaller place where your dog can be kept safe and away from anything in the house he could damage when left alone. The crate door can, therefore, be left open at all times and the dog can choose to go to his 'den', but is never forced to stay there. Like this it can be a 'safe area' for a dog to hide away from possible threats, as well as a great place to escape to, from other members of the household such as pets or children.

This crate would be suitable for a smaller dog, such as a Jack Russell terrier. The towels placed on top of the crate add to its 'den'-like appeal, and a thick jumper and toys inside help to make it an inviting place to go to.

CASE STUDY – A SAFE PLACE

Marley was a very frightened year-old male labrador who had been found as a stray. He came into Vanessa's home for only one night, and immediately hid under a bookshelf. He was so frightened that he tried to get into the smallest areas, as these were the only places he felt safe. As soon as a crate was set up he crawled straight inside and Vanessa covered it over so that he would feel safe and secure. He spent most of the night there and Vanessa ensured that there were no human comings and goings so he could feel safe. Without the crate, he would have found the night in the home environment a great deal more frightening.

This dog found the bottom of this bookcase the safest place until a crate was set up. His crate was essential for him to feel secure.

CASE STUDY – AN ANXIOUS PLACE

Bennie is a four-year-old cross-breed terrier male, and was very energetic in the home, running and playing from room to room, reluctant to settle and relax. His owners came across an article on crates, and decided that a crate would help Bennie to stay calm and less active during the day. In spite of no previous crate training and a reluctance to go into it, Bennie was crated for three to four hours during the day and was also confined overnight.

Not long after the frequent crating Bennie began to jump up and nip his owners. Moreover, his activity levels increased dramatically, leading his owners to confine him for longer periods. Eventually he was so difficult to handle that his owners asked Vanessa for help.

As the initial reason for crating had been to influence his activity levels and calm his behaviour in the home, Vanessa advised them to allow him free access to the crate in a smaller area of the house at night and when the owners went out. Bennie was also given some training to shape the nipping behaviour, and some relaxation training.

Confining a dog does not necessarily mean they will be calmer and relaxed, in fact the opposite may occur, as was the case with Bennie. Crating prevents a dog from getting any exercise or freedom to express his normal behaviours, and can cause numerous side effects. When Bennie was allowed to make that all-important 'choice' of whether or not to go into the crate, he chose the crate much more readily and was increasingly able to relax.

A dog with separation anxieties should never be put in a crate, as you are effectively reaffirming everything he is frightened of, and can make his concern a great deal worse. The idea that his crate is 'safe and secure' is only true if he has had time to develop this feeling about it. If you confine him in a crate and leave him alone without any prior training he will never be able to make this association. However, if you want to confine your new dog before you have worked on crate use, put the crate in a room with the door closed, or with a stair gate blocking the entrance.

Many adult rescue dogs, particularly strays or those who have had little human contact, have never been crate trained. It is important to establish a positive association with the crate by giving your dog the choice of whether or not he goes there. An open door whether your dog is inside or out is always more inviting than one that is locked and bolted.

While the word 'crate' is much less offensive than the word 'cage', they have a very similar appearance, and being human, we associate many of the negative images from our culture with them. To dogs, however, a cage is just another object to explore. This is why it is essential that you allow your dog to do just that. Ensure that the 'crate' becomes an interesting and relaxing place to seek out, by placing new toys, treats or even his meals in there for him to discover. Regarding it as his 'den' rather than as a 'sin bin' should prevent you from both negative use and negative associations.

Before you buy a crate you need to measure your dog's height as well as his length. Measure his height when standing from the floor to the top of his head, and add four to five inches. It should be large enough for the dog to stand up, turn round, lie down comfortably and stretch out to sleep. If you believe your dog is likely to grow, then you might opt for a crate with dividers.

Some Hints for Crate Use

It should not be necessary to confine your dog to a crate, but if for some reason it is, then keep it to short periods of time: an hour is a long time to be restricted to such a small space. Training your dog to be left in the crate can take time, and should be done very gradually.

- Place his bedding in the crate so he becomes accustomed to sleeping in there with the door open.
- Decide on a command to guide your dog to his crate area: for example 'den'.
- When your dog goes in and out of the crate willingly (which may take weeks!) close the door for a few seconds or a minute, and stay near by.
- Do not wait for him to show he wants to come out; a minute is long enough.
- Let him out calmly.
- Wait for a few minutes, and repeat the exercise again. Over the course of a week continue this exercise and gradually increase the time he is in the crate

with the door shut.
- To get him accustomed to staying in the crate, give him meals or treats in the crate with the door open.
- Put some washable bedding and a toy in the crate for comfort.
- The first few times you leave him should be less than fifteen minutes. When you are ready to leave him longer, you could leave a tape recorder with him so you will know if he is howling or barking. This is a sign of fear or anxiety, as is damage to the crate or to surroundings objects and evidence of drooling, salivating, urinating or defecating in the crate. If any of these occur you should seek help.

Stair Gates

If you do not have the space or income, or if you simply don't want to get a crate, then you might consider a stair gate. These are useful for confining your dog to a particular room or part of the house without shutting him in a small space; he can still see people coming and going, but his freedom to roam everywhere is restricted. Gates can be useful anywhere; for instance you can place a gate in the hall doorway so the dog can't reach the front door when visitors arrive, which is especially helpful in the early days when he is settling in.

Stair gates can often be bought in charity shops for a few pounds, or in shops catering for infants. Before buying one, check that your dog cannot jump over it, knock it down or get his head caught in the bars.

Using a stair gate to restrict access is significantly less stressful for the dog than crating, and requires less training. However, it is important to prepare the room in which the dog is to be contained from the dog's perspective, ensuring you

A stair gate can be very effective in helping you confine a dog to a smaller area of a house, or to prevent him going into certain areas. The gate in this photograph is separating two rooms in the house.

ensure that neither the squeaker nor the soft filling inside the toy are discovered and swallowed. Check these toys regularly, and throw away any that have been chewed so much that they could be dangerous.

It is also necessary to abandon that cosy image of a happy dog settling down to chew a large bone, because natural bones should be avoided as they have a tendency to splinter into sharp, dangerous pieces. It is better to buy artificially flavoured bones (liver, chicken, bacon) which are designed to be chewed for hours and do not break up into small pieces. Likewise beware of using sticks in that favourite game of fetch, as many an unfortunate dog has been rushed to the vet to remove splinters from his mouth or throat. There are even documented cases of dogs being impaled and seriously injured when a stick has bounced back.

Rawhide chews are also potentially dangerous, as they can break off into

remove any items he might damage or chew.

Toys

Toys are very important for fulfilling a number of needs: they help dogs to chew, tug, shake, toss, carry, hide and bury, without your home or your possessions being destroyed. They also prevent boredom, and as such should be rotated to maintain interest. There are, of course several important considerations.

Before you buy any toy, make sure it is safe: it should not have toxic colouring, or loose bits that can fall off or break, or parts that the dog could chew or swallow such as strings, eyes or ribbons; and it should not be so small that the dog could swallow it whole. Soft and squeaky toys are fun but should be supervised to

Both these dogs are very interested in this blue rubber ring. Even the simplest toys can generate chewing and playing opportunities.

small chunks, which can scratch or puncture your dog's gastrointestinal tract. Moreover when the rawhide becomes very moist it becomes thick and sticky, and could get stuck in his throat. There are non-rawhide-based chew strips available, which are a safer alternative.

Using household items such as socks, shoes, treated wood, cardboard boxes, plastic bottles and so on as toys should be avoided for two reasons. Firstly, he cannot be expected to know which household items he is allowed to play with and which he is not, so costly mistakes are possible. Secondly, some of the materials used in these items contain toxic chemicals or can be easily shredded and swallowed. Similarly, buying toys in the shape of your possessions such as shoes or socks is not advisable as the dog has no way of distinguishing between them and the real thing.

Safe Toys

Toys that would be safe playthings include cotton rope toys, Kongs® and puzzle toys. Cotton rope toys are usually twisted and knotted at both ends to make a bone shape, and are good for pulling and tugging games; they are best used under supervision. Kongs® are hard rubber chew toys in a variety of shapes with a hollow centre, which can be stuffed with treats and fillings. Puzzle toys, such as treat balls, can be filled with dry treats such as dog biscuits; the ball is pierced with strategically placed holes, and the dog must roll the toy around so the treats fall out at random from the holes.

Treat balls together with a stuffed Kong make excellent entertainment for

Giving a dog a boot to play with is not such a good idea as it will encourage him to play with other footwear – and a few minutes' chewing will do a lot of damage to a pair of high heels!

Balls make excellent toys for dogs, and most pet shops stock a variety of rubber balls specially designed for them.

Giles is focused intently on the ball about to be thrown for him. Balls can be used as a way to attract attention and positively reinforce behaviour. If Giles is asked to 'sit' and, as he does so, the ball is given to him, the 'sit' is positively reinforced.

If you have more than one dog, ensure there are plenty of toys to go round.

many dogs. However, dogs that become easily frustrated will only become more anxious if they have to 'work' for their food, so they are best given straightforward play items, or food they can eat easily.

FOOD

For the first two weeks it is advisable to continue feeding your dog the same food as he was used to in the re-homing centre, and keep to the same feeding schedule. This is one change that he does not need to have. Just think how comforting we find the familiar 'nice cup of tea' when we are unsettled or unhappy. He may not even want to eat for the first day, but don't worry; simply remove the untouched food after twenty minutes, and don't try again until the next feeding time. (This also applies to picky eaters.)

Do not disturb your dog while he is eating, and if he shows any potentially aggressive behaviour during feeding, ensure you move away and call him into a different area of the house, keeping him separate from his food station before picking up his bowl. Such behaviour may be caused by a learnt response as a result of him being deprived of sufficient food supplies at some point in his life. It is, however, advisable to seek professional help, as behaviour modification will require sensitive handling, and a full assessment must be conducted before training begins. It is also advisable to take him for a veterinary check to ensure there are no medical factors influencing this behaviour.

Do not be tempted to feed your dog titbits while you are eating, as you will soon have him drooling by your dinner plate. This practice can also lead to an overweight dog, and it may result in sanitary accidents as the urine and defecation cycle will be disrupted.

CHOCOLATE CAN KILL

Never give your dog chocolate. Even small amounts can be toxic, causing a rapid heartbeat, collapse and in some cases death.

Look for a food that uses quality ingredients and contains fewer by-products to bulk it out, and no preservatives as these can trigger food allergies. If your dog suffers from digestive problems such as diarrhoea or constipation, or has allergies, it is vital that you take him to your vet for professional advice. A suitable diet is important to a dog's physical and psychological wellbeing, and can make a huge difference to his behaviour; furthermore there are special diets specifically designed for behaviour concerns. However, any special diet must be supervised by your vet and behaviourist.

Dry food helps keep the teeth cleaner, and is good for the digestion.

The daily diet can be supplemented with fresh vegetables such as green beans and baby carrots; the frozen variety of these are soothing chews. Many dogs enjoy chewing and eating vegetables such as carrots just as much as they enjoy devouring the same size meat treat out of a packet. Avoid coloured treats or chews, as these often contain unnecessary additives. It is also important to be aware that some bones, especially chicken bones, can splinter easily, and shards of bone can lodge in the dog's

Dry food and dog chews can help to maintain the health of your dog's teeth and gums.

throat or stomach and cause fatal punctures; rubber bones are a safe alternative.

Chewing is an important part of a dog's life, and literally makes him feel good as it leads to the brain producing mood-enhancing chemicals. This is especially useful to dogs that suffer from stress.

GROOMING

Grooming is important for the following reasons:

- Health: Through regular grooming you become familiar with your dog so you will be able to notice any changes in his skin, ears, mouth and body.
- Bonding: Grooming is a good way to bond with your dog, so you should try to make it as pleasant as possible.
- Aesthetics: Grooming will make your dog look and smell nicer, so he will be

as appealing to your friends as to you.
- Home hygiene: Regular brushing removes dead skin and hair that will otherwise end up on furniture and floors.

After a bath or playing in water, your dog will need to be dried, and towel drying, like brushing, must be introduced gradually with positive reinforcement and awareness of your dog's signals: if he freezes, stares, glares, growls or becomes concerned, stop what you are doing and allow him to dry naturally.

Individual Grooming Requirements
A smooth-coated dog will require at least weekly grooming; a rough or long-coated dog will need more. Even short-haired breeds must have regular brushing to remove excess hair to allow the skin to breath. If necessary trim the hair around the genitals, anus and belly so that dirt

and waste have no place to cling. Protect your home by brushing outdoors, particularly when he is shedding his coat. Some longer-haired breeds such as poodles, spaniels, setters, bearded collies, many terrier types and various cross-breeds may benefit from professional grooming, when their coat is trimmed and managed.

Your dog may not enjoy his grooming routine at first, so you will need to introduce the process slowly: give positive rewards, such as a tasty treat or praise, when he is calm and confident and happy to be brushed, and start off with a soft brush, which he will find soothing and will make his coat shine. When he is used to this, you can introduce a hard wire brush and/or comb, as this is the only way to remove debris and tangles.

Brushes must be strong enough to stand up to tangles without breaking, but fine enough to root out fleas, seeds

The young puppy requires drying after a play in the field. Some rescue dogs dislike such handling, possibly due to a negative experience in the past.

The large black dog is unlikely to need professional grooming; the spaniel in front of him, however, is very likely to need regular clipping.

and so on. Start at his head and work your way to his tail, checking for any signs of parasites, unusual skin growths or mats of hair along the way. The ears should be checked for dirt, infection or parasites. You can gently wipe dirt from the outer ear, but do not go any deeper as you could damage his hearing.

Parasites or infections should be dealt with by a vet. Burrs can be removed by first saturating them with white petroleum jelly or mineral oil, then work them out of your dog's hair with your hands.

It is also important to keep your dog's nails trimmed, not only to make him more comfortable when he is walking and exercising, but to avoid painful infections and ingrown nails. If you are nervous about doing this job, get the rescue centre or your vet to show you how. Regularly clipped nails will be less likely to split or to shred your upholstery or other fabric.

Grooming Tools

Long, thick hair needs brushes with bristles that are farther apart, such as pin brushes. Short hair requires shorter,

This brush has soft bristles and is an ideal first brush to use. Avoid spiky bristles to start with until your dog has grown in confidence.

harder bristles. An alternative to a brush is a grooming glove that you wear on your hand; the tiny prongs on the glove's surface remove dead hair as you gently stroke your dog. A damp rubber glove will help remove excess hair from your dog as well as your furniture.

Dog toenail clippers come in scissor or guillotine style; the latter leaves no margin for error. If you are at all concerned about clipping your dog's nails take him to the vet because mistakes can be hazardous for the dog.

Most dogs love being brushed. If your dog doesn't, don't worry – just take time to develop his confidence so he learns that it is an enjoyable activity.

7 CHILDREN AND DOGS

The arrival of your rescue dog will affect every member of the family in some way. Everyone should be happy to live with the dog so that he can feel safe and secure and one of the family; the children in particular will no doubt be very happy to welcome a new dog into their home. The question is, will the dog be happy to meet your children?

This chapter will help you to ensure that he is by explaining the relationship between children and dogs, and showing you how to prepare them for the dog's arrival. The way a child treats a dog is critical in a successful re-homing.

Many of the books that deal with this topic take the view that you should train your dog to be safe with children. This is totally reasonable, but dog ownership is a two-way relationship and we believe it is equally important to train your children to be safe with dogs.

Many dogs find themselves in re-homing centres because they have become unsociable with the children in their home. This can be soul-destroying for both the family and the dog, and we aim to show how to reduce the possibility of this happening. To begin with, ensure that both parties are starting off with a 'level playing field': so the first question you should ask about a dog you are

Dogs can add so much to a family. Prepare your home and family before you bring your rescue dog home, and you will be set for success and a wonderful future with your new companion.

considering is, 'Have you evidence that he is good with children?'

In the absence of positive evidence, no one can be sure how a dog will react on a day-to-day basis. If there is no evidence that he is sociable with children, or the re-homing centre feels he is not a suitable candidate, do not take the chance; save everyone from possible heartache and find another dog.

WHY DO YOU WANT A DOG?

Parents offer many reasons for wanting a dog for their child. Many feel that owning a dog can teach their child responsibility; others may have been nagged by their children for months or even years; some parents want their child to experience the same love and companionship that they had with their own childhood dog.

The first reason is worthy, but places unrealistic expectations on both the child and the dog. A child is a child, and needs a whole range of learning experiences to allow him to develop into a rounded adult. Placing the whole burden of dog ownership on his young shoulders is unfair and isolating. It is vital from the outset that every member of the family is involved in caring for and house training their new dog – but more of that later.

If you are about to give in to your child's nagging, then cast your mind back to all the other things they begged and pleaded for, things they were certain would make them happy – and then just try to remember how long that bit of happiness lasted. The fact of the matter is that a dog is a living, breathing creature that may be adorable but also needs a great deal of work and commitment.

Although many children plead for a dog of their own and will promise to walk and care for him, the reality can be somewhat different. Many children may not be able to give this commitment as their situation is likely to change substantially from the early days of owning a dog: school and university are two major components that may reduce the time an older child has to offer. The parents will be the primary carer for the dog's entire life, although their children can be very important 'assistants'.

In fact unless you are 100 per cent ready to love and care for a dog yourself, delay your decision until you have finished reading this book.

Finally, wanting to re-home a dog so that all family members can experience the same love and companionship you

Lizzy, who is standing with Giles, assists her grandparents who are his owners, by loving him and playing with him.

felt with a previous childhood dog is sound motivation. It suggests that at least one member of the family has an understanding of dogs and realistic expectations of the work involved.

THE ADVANTAGES TO CHILDREN

Improved Health

It is easy to see how playing with or walking a dog can improve overall fitness for everybody concerned. This is particularly important in times of increasing childhood obesity, which is often exacerbated by addiction to television and computer games. However, there are other benefits that are not generally known. A study carried out in 2004 found that children whose family owned a pet had an extra eighteen half-days at school over the course of the year compared to those without animals. The researchers found the antibody levels among pet-owning children were significantly more stable, meaning that they had stronger immune systems. In other words, getting down and dirty with their pets was far better than living in a controlled, antiseptic environment[10].

Improved Quality of Life

Children today are under considerable pressure to perform well, not only at school but also in their leisure activities. Parents try their best to give their unconditional love, but so great is the pressure to be model parents that it would be miraculous if some anxiety did not leak out. For a large number of children their dog is their one true friend.

A study conducted in Germany found that 80 per cent of the children interviewed felt their dog was an important friend and confidante, while 90 per cent of the parents thought that the family dog played an important role in teaching their young children social skills and improved the child's quality of life. In another survey of 338 children, it was found that 40 per cent of children sought out their dog if they were upset, and 85 per cent regarded their dogs as a playmate[11].

Among the wealth of research on pet ownership and children the following claims have been made about pets such as dogs:

- They can be safe recipients of secrets and private thoughts – children often talk to their pets, as they do to their animal toys.
- They provide lessons about life: reproduction, birth, illnesses, accidents, death and bereavement.
- They can help develop responsible behaviour in the children who care for them.
- They provide a connection to nature.
- They can teach respect for other living things.

However, all this does not happen by simply putting children and dogs together and letting them get on with it.

TEACHING AND LEARNING

Both children and dogs learn in two ways:

- By observing their own species – social and observational learning.
- By trying things out – empirical learning.

Sadly for the dog, we often separate him from his own species so he must rely on our good sense to ensure that he can hold his head high in the doggy world and pass muster in ours. What both human and canine species share is an intense awareness of the world around them. For the child, the centre of their world is their parents or carers, and what they do and how they do it is accepted wholeheartedly.

Thus the burden of responsibility for your child's learning rests squarely on your adult shoulders. If you use brutal training methods and punishment to train your dog, you teach your children that violence is an acceptable means to an end. However, if you show your dog care and understanding, establish clear instructions and use positive reinforcement and unconditional love, your child will learn to respect not only animals but people as well.

The second way that both your child and your dog learn what is acceptable in your home is by remembering the result of their actions. If you lavishly praise your dog when he sits for the first time, and do the same to your child when he is gentle with the dog, then both are likely to repeat the behaviour because they will remember that it results in praise.

Similarly, children learn that if they are gentle and kind to their dog they will be rewarded by his companionship. By seeing the effect of their actions on the dog, they are likely to develop empathy, and to generalize this from their dog to people. Research has shown that children with pets at home are more socially competent, more popular, feel better about themselves, and are better able to understand other children's feelings[12].

'IT'S ALL RIGHT, SHE'S USED TO IT'

A family visited a rescue centre wanting to re-home their German shepherd as they had a two-year-old child and were expecting another baby very soon. As the dog was very nervous, an assessment was necessary before accepting her. She clearly adored every member of the family, especially the two-year-old child who, to everyone's amusement, was flailing a broom handle she had found and was narrowly missing the assessment staff with it. But their amusement turned to concern as she turned her attention to the German shepherd, and very nearly struck the dog. To the assessment staff's dismay the parents responded to the gasps of horror by saying dismissively, 'It's all right; she's used to it!'

What a sad state of affairs. In spite of having a nervous disposition, this dog had never reacted defensively to any of this family's behaviour, even when she had been 'bitten and had her ears pulled' by the child. The parents seemed unaware that they had been courting disaster, as their two-year-old could have been injured. It was quite irrelevant that the dog was used to this treatment and did not react. When a dog is hurt and made to feel pain, there are few responses at his disposal: he can try to show appeasement behaviour or move away, but when this repeatedly does not work, common sense dictates he will try something else. He can give a warning growl or show his teeth, he can nip to tell the individual to 'back off', and if all else fails he may use his teeth a little harder to get the point across. This behaviour is particularly concerning with children because they may not notice the 'early warning signs', which are critical.

It is not acceptable to allow any human, however young, to disrespect an animal by hurting it. This is a fundamental lesson that all children should be taught, regardless of age. If you fail to teach this lesson, then your child will have missed an important part of his or her socialization. What is more, you are risking that your dog may harm your child, a risk that need not arise.

NATURAL BEHAVIOURS

Some behaviour is so important for the survival of the species that it is hard-wired into the brain. Humans are able to override instinctive behaviours, as is shown by those who go on hunger strikes. However, in spite of years of human interference, certain behaviours are hard-wired to such an extent in the dog's brain that they have survived to some degree in all breeds. If we want our dogs to become our companions, we must teach our children about these behaviours so they understand and respect them.

Dogs have evolved from predatory ancestors, which existed by hunting almost anything including small mammals, birds, snakes, fish, insects and even earthworms. Although selective breeding has reduced their predatory

Dogs commonly use each other as 'prey' figures, and enjoy chasing and grabbing in mock games. The two dogs in this photograph are participating in just such a game, and are very much enjoying themselves.

behaviour, it is still part of their genetic make-up. Many of the games we play with our dogs – from stick throwing to tug-of-war – utilize these prey behaviours.

If circumstances allow, dogs may try to catch actual prey such as cats, squirrels, sheep or rabbits. Although they are less likely to indulge in predatory behaviour with animals to which they have been socialized, these instincts are easily aroused by fast movement and high-pitched noise. These happen to be two behaviours that almost define childhood. A running child may trigger the chase response in a dog's brain. This is a chemical stimulus rather than a rational thought, and many dogs become very excited and rough, displaying 'over the top' behaviour through play to predator mode very quickly. This is one of the reasons why it is important never to leave any dog alone with a child.

Young children often regard their dog as they would a toy, and as far as they are concerned the dog has no feelings. What is more, a heavy diet of cartoon entertainment can leave a child convinced that you can bash a dog on the head, punch him under the chin and squash him into dustbins, without any chance of serious injury. Children have a tendency to tug on dogs' ears, pull on their tails or jump on their backs, and some children even love to scream in a sleeping dog's ear, or persist in chasing them. It only takes one of these actions to inflict pain or make your dog feel threatened, and it could possibly lead to him displaying defensive or aggressive behaviour. Teach your children how to behave around dogs (and vice versa), but ensure you are present at all times to monitor the situation.

Boys between the ages of five and nine are bitten by dogs five times more than

KEEPING ONE STEP AHEAD

Avoid conflicts by preventing your children from behaving in a threatening way towards your dog. Equally, ensure that your children are aware of the signals your dog uses to show he is unhappy, fearful or frustrated. If your dog freezes, stares, glares, growls or shows any of his teeth, your child must stop what he is doing and back away.

These dogs are involved in some very rough play. Misunderstandings can arise if your child plays rough games with a newly rehomed rescue dog, so it is advisable to leave this kind of play to the dogs.

any other group of people. Their noisy and physical play can simulate many of the behaviours that young dogs exhibit when playing, which often involves mouthing and biting. While mouthing and play biting between dog brothers can be fairly harmless, a dog mouthing or biting a human boy can be much more serious. If you hear shouting, banging and excited barking, get out there fast and calm everyone down. Also make sure that your child understands that he should play quietly with his dog, at least until they know each other better.

COMMUNICATION

A significant part of a dog's communication with other dogs is focused on personal safety, personal space and personal belongings. One signal that dogs can interpret as a threat to their personal safety is direct, 'staring' eye contact. Unfortunately, children are inclined to stare intently at animals, and the dog may interpret this as a threat. It is important that parents explain to their children that their dog is likely to be upset by such intense eye contact, and so they mustn't do it.

In addition it should be stressed that if the dog shows any 'warning' signals, such as growling or showing his teeth, they must stop what they are doing. If they don't, the dog may be 'forced' to retaliate by growling, nipping, snapping or biting to keep them away.

A great deal of a dog's genetic behaviour is devoted to seeking and obtaining food. As considerable effort is invested to this end, it is not difficult to imagine how a dog's instinct to defend his food may be particularly sharp. This is especially so if food has ever been scarce, as can be the case with rescue dogs who have been strays. Consequently, there are many reports of children being bitten when a dog felt the child was threatening to take his food.

A huge dose of common sense is needed here. Why should your child pester the dog when he is eating? Many dogs clear their bowls within minutes, therefore ask the child to leave the dog to eat in peace for that length of time. Also take care that your child waits until he has walked away from his feeding area and the bowl is removed before interacting with him.

A comforting piece of advice is, don't expect your dog to be perfect, and don't test him by trying to take away his food while he is eating. Toys can be another source of contention – although they needn't be! Just ensure your child doesn't 'steal' toys or chews from the dog – there is no point in such actions. If he wants to play with the dog, use the 'swapping game' in a polite manner: by holding out a different toy you can entice the dog to join in the children's play. Every dog is different, and relationships need to be well developed before either party can

It is difficult for us to tell which of these toys is for a dog and which is for a child, so imagine how difficult it must be from the dog's point of view. To make things simpler for all concerned, separate the two.

'take' items away from the other – and even then it is advisable to teach both your dog and your child to be 'polite' when doing this.

It would be one less job for you if your child were 'officially' and 'formally' appointed 'toy monitor', and was made responsible for keeping his playthings out of your dog's reach. All that would then be needed was to be sure that your dog's toys are different from the children's toys: the dog can't be expected to know the difference between his brown furry teddy and your daughter's pink and white furry Bagpuss, because as far as he is concerned they are both soft toys.

Having said all this, it would be a huge mistake to encourage a protective approach to his food bowl or toys. If any concerning resource-guarding tendencies are shown, behaviour modification may be necessary through professional guidance.

Don't confuse your dog by giving him objects such as old children's toys or socks that closely resemble items that are 'off limits'. He can't tell the difference, and when he starts trotting round the house with your lingerie in his mouth, you'll only have yourself to blame!

Rougher Play Games

As dog owners, we are often delighted to join in any game that our dog initiates. One such game is 'tug-of-war', which can develop out of a game of 'fetch' but can also begin by merely flapping a rag or suchlike in the dog's direction, and holding on while he tries to pull it from us. However, this is not an advisable game with a dog you do not know, as participants can get too overwrought; if your dog becomes too over-excited, with growling behaviour, take a break and do something else. It is certainly not advisable for young children to play this game, as many dogs reach higher up the toy and can get too close to hands and arms.

Establishing a Positive Association

It is essential that your dog has a positive association with your children, and this can be achieved by 'positively reinforcing' him with rewards such as tasty treats or toys when they are around. If your child can give him a treat, this is all the better. However, children can be afraid of being bitten when handing the reward to their dog, so they jerk their hand away at the last second. The dog may then jump up or lunge towards them, which can result in the child being knocked down. Teach the child to place the treat in an open palm, rather than holding it in his fingers. You can help him to do this by placing your hand under his.

If your child is still likely to be nervous,

See how this dog's head is at the same height as the child's. Many dogs will seem very large and frightening to an uncertain child, and are often just the right height to knock them over.

you can ask him to give you the treat to give to your dog. This secondary positive reinforcement works wonderfully well when either party is a little nervous. The dog is able to see and smell that the treats came from the child, but is not forced into taking it from someone he is unsure of, or vice versa.

A dog's head is often at the same height as the child's, so many dogs are going to appear larger and potentially more frightening to an uncertain child, and furthermore are often just the right height to easily knock a child over. This highlights the importance of teaching both your child and your dog how to behave with each other so that a successful relationship can be developed.

Ten Rules

It is important that your child learns that he must not do the following:

1. Poke your dog's eyes, mouth, or inside his ears.
2. Pull your dog's tail or legs.
3. Run around your dog if he is getting over-excited.
4. Shout around your dog.
5. Disturb your dog when he is in his bed or quiet area.
6. Touch your dog or his food when he is eating.
7. Shout near your dog while he is sleeping, as dogs can become frightened if they are woken up suddenly.
8. Hug your new dog around the neck. Some dogs do not like being grabbed around the neck as it can make them fearful and potentially defensive.
9. Stroke or pat your new dog without asking: curl your fingers under and let him sniff the back of your hand first.
10. Do not stay near your dog if he freezes, stares, growls, lifts his lips,

backs away or raises the hair on his back. It is very important that all members of the family, but especially children, know to do this.

This is a lot of information to digest, but it is important that it is all passed on to your children – and there are various ways that this might be done. For a start, children under seven cannot be expected to retain all this information in the abstract. However, while you are preparing your home for the dog, you can explain what you are doing and why. In this way you should aim to emphasize the following points:

- A new dog may be easily frightened, so everyone must be very gentle with him.
- He has special ways of doing everything (eating, going to the toilet, playing), so it is important to learn how he does them, and to make it easy for him.

Once you bring your dog home you need to supervise your children's interactions with the dog, gently showing them how to handle him and interpreting his movements for them. In this way your child will digest the rules unconsciously.

Older children, on the other hand, will want to prepare more actively for the new arrival. They will easily digest the rules if you can present them in an enjoyable way. Here are a few ideas that depend for their success on the nature of your child.

- They can write or tell a story in which, for example, a mother dog warns her puppies about children; or where one heroic child saves a poor dog from an immoral gang that does everything wrong.
- Children who don't enjoy writing stories could use the Internet to make a project. Ask them to search key words from the list of rules, and cut and paste what they find into text. However, they must be able to read and understand what they have written. Blindly copying everything is totally without value, although sadly many children have been led to believe that twenty pages of unintelligible waffle is superior to five pages of words they can understand.
- If they enjoy drawing, they could make a huge poster of the rules on a sheet of wallpaper. The rules can be illustrated with pictures from magazines, Clipart or best of all their own drawings.
- If they are not keen to write or draw, you can help them to design a board game where you race against time to get the happiest family dog. At the roll of the dice you might land on a square that says: 'You scared your dog by playing football with your friends in the garden. Go back three places!' Another square may say: 'Your dog is very happy that you left him alone while he had his food. Go forward two places!' As with designing a poster, illustrations will add to the enjoyment.

If you want your new dog to become a part of your child's life, discussion and planning are necessary to help make dog ownership a positive experience for everyone. A child who learns to care for a dog, and treats him kindly and patiently, is well on the way to becoming the sort of adult who is reliable, sensible and a pleasure to know.

8 DOGS, GARDENS AND THEIR MUTUAL PROTECTION

When you bring your new dog home he will want to explore your garden – but the question is, will they be ready for each other? The two main issues arising are the safety of the dog and the destruction of the garden – but you don't need to choose between them. In this chapter we will explain how to make your existing garden safe for the dog, and then how to protect it from the dog.

GARDEN CHECKLIST

Potential dog owners should ensure their garden is safe and secure before they bring a dog home, rather than adopting a 'fire-fighting' approach after his arrival. In fact it is very unlikely you will 'pass' a home visit from the re-homing centre if your garden is not fully secure, as this is an essential requirement for most of them.

The re-homing centre will be anxious that in preparing your garden for your dog you have fulfilled the following criteria:

- If you already have fences, check them for gaps and replace any rotten or splintered wood: many expensive injuries have resulted from dogs chewing these. If the fence is less than 6ft (1.8m) high, ask the re-homing centre if the dog you are having would be able to jump over it.

A section of a securely fenced garden: the fence has no gaps or holes in it, and is over 5ft (1.5m) in height.

AN IMPORTANT CONSIDERATION

Toxicariasis is a parasitic infection caused by roundworms that infect dogs and cats. The larvae are excreted in their faeces. Children can get infected with toxicariasis when playing in areas where dogs have been to the toilet. Symptoms can include fever, coughing or wheezing, skin rash and even problems with vision. Sandboxes should be covered when not in use, and children should be taught always to wash their hands carefully after playing outside, and never to put their dirty hands in their mouth. Regular worming helps to lessen the chance of a dog getting toxicariasis.

- Make sure the gate closes properly and there is no space for your new dog to squeeze under.
- Gravel paths can hurt his paws; washed pea gravel is better and forest bark is a cheaper alternative. However, as dogs can disturb paths of bark mulch or pea gravel, paths of brick or stone are easier to maintain.
- Fence off or cover ponds and water gardens as these can be serious hazards.
- Avoid cocoa bean mulch as dogs are very sensitive to theobromine found in cocoa beans, cocoa bean hulls and chocolate.
- Store all garden chemicals in plastic containers with secure lids where your dog will not be able to get inside them.
- Remove citronella candles and slug bait, which can be toxic, as well as traps of any kind.
- Tidy away all garden tools and get into the habit of doing this straight after use.
- Decking may need re-sanding to prevent splinters getting into your dog's feet.
- Be prepared to provide shade and a drink in hot weather. While a leafy tree and a shallow pond would be lovely, a cheap sun umbrella and bowl of water will be just as effective.

Experienced home-checkers are often surprised how some very obvious dangers are missed by prospective owners, particularly those who have previously owned a dog. Don't assume that your new dog will not try to jump over your low fence just because your previous dog didn't. Even if you do not have a home check, remember that prevention is better than cure: an afternoon spent repairing the hole in your fence is better than a day spent searching your local woods for your new dog which has no idea where he is, let alone how to find his way back home.

A secure garden is essential; larch-lap fences are fairly reasonably priced and prevent passers-by from teasing your dogs or risking bitten fingers by poking them through the slats. If it would be too expensive to fence the whole garden, fence an area for the dog. Such an area is an advantage at night as you can simply take him to it and leave him to go to the toilet without having to hang around waiting for him. A dog run should be at least 3m (10ft) wide and as long as possible so the dog can run up and down and exercise in safety. Bury the bottom of the fence or chicken wire about 8in (20cm) under the ground to stop him digging his way out. Shrubs or other plants placed close together along the fence may also deter escape attempts.

This young puppy has discovered the pond, which is a significant hazard to a young and inquisitive dog. It is important that such areas are covered or fenced off, especially if the water is deep or full of fish that you do not want to be disturbed.

'How high can your dog jump?' The lurcher in this photograph is finding this barrier no match for his jumping ability.

One of Vanessa's clients was a small female terrier, an escape artist par excellence, that refused to return to her owner's call. On her first consultation the motivation for the terrier's behaviour was clear: the garden was situated next to a woodland with a generous quantity of birdlife and a river. Moreover, it didn't take Vanessa long to discover a large number of holes and gaps in the fence and hedge that were worn smooth by frequent exits and entrances! A rustle in the trees, followed by the alarm call of a pheasant was all it took for the terrier to jump through a gap and disappear.

All that was needed in order to limit, if not resolve the problem, was the erection of a secure fence: without an effective boundary the dog found it impossible to ignore her instincts, and was rushing off after any possible prey. This simple solution prevented the problem arising in the first place. However, refusing to return when called took more time to resolve (see Chapter 14).

Bear in mind that even smaller dogs may be able to jump or climb over fences, so it is vital to ensure there are no gaps in your fence, and also that it is high enough for the dog you are about to re-home. A determined dog may not need to jump over the fence; a gap in the gateway may be all he needs. Ensure that gateways are fully enclosed and gates are of adequate height.

Resist the temptation to tie up your dog to stop him escaping; he will risk strangling himself and it will cause him undue stress, while his barking may be classed as noise pollution. A large majority of calls to re-homing centres come from people living next to a dog that barks all day long because he is shut out in the garden.

Quite apart from these obvious welfare and nuisance issues, there are people out there looking for the opportunity to steal dogs; if yours is left alone in the garden with nobody at home, there is a much higher chance that you could be a victim of this crime. This may also put him at risk from potential tormentors made aware of his location by his whines, cries or barks.

GARDENING WITH YOUR DOG IN MIND

Both dogs and foxes seem to think that fertilizers, bone meal, blood meal or fish emulsion smell fantastic, and both are likely to start digging to find the treat. Be prepared for this if you are determined to use them. It would be difficult for a keen gardener to avoid the use of pesticides and fertilizers, but to minimize their effect on your dog and children, apply them when there is no wind or rain forecast for a day or two.

Keep both your dog and children

inside when applying either pesticides or fertilizers, and keep them off treated lawns for twenty-four hours. Nitrogen-based lawn fertilizers can burn the pads on your dog's feet. Always follow the instructions on the product's label.

Find a safe alternative to those blue metaldehyde slug pellets which are dangerous to animals if eaten.

Finally, be warned that stretched wire meant to deter birds or support crops can garrotte your dog as well as humans. If you use wire supports in your fruit garden make sure he cannot run into them.

Most dogs are unlikely to chew your plants, but just in case, it is advisable to keep him away from the following:

- Tomatoes, green peppers, potatoes, petunias and the eggplant: all these contain various amounts of neurotoxic alkaloids which act directly on the nervous system. Their cousins, daturas and nightshades, which are annual plants spread by birds, contain more concentrated amounts of poisons.
- Daffodil, foxglove, delphinium, bittersweet, wisteria, lupin, buttercup, dicentra, morning glory and periwinkle will cause vomiting and diarrhoea if nibbled.

SAVING YOUR GARDEN FROM YOUR DOG

Dogs can be a nightmare in a landscaped garden. They urinate on lawns or shrubs, roll in flowers, chew on vegetables and branches, and dig holes.

Garden Design Tips

The more informal your garden, the less noticeable will be the presence of your

This dog is perfectly safe in this informal garden. The wooden fence is set flush with the ground, and the roots of established bushes and perennials make it difficult for her to dig. Large trees act as focal points and make flowerbeds redundant.

dog. Large trees and shrubs take the eye away from the smaller details, and established clumps of perennials are less vulnerable to damage from balls and jumping than are those newly bought from garden centres. Grouping taller plants together will encourage your dog to go round them, rather than force his way through.

If you want really tough and low maintenance plants, go for ornamental grasses such as the slender metre-high feather reed grass, or purple moor grass which also adds texture to herbaceous perennials. Use a wire mesh enclosure to protect small trees.

Holes

You could also limit the time you spend weeding, as well as preventing digging, by having as little bare soil as possible. Plant perennials close together, and use tough ground cover such as thyme, cotoneaster, creeping phlox or even

Close-planted evergreen shrubs discourage dogs from amateur gardening. The density of the planting makes damage from thrown balls less likely.

roses. Sturdy perennials include verbena, coneflower, black-eyed Susans, Shasta daisy, Liriope, Russian sage and Mexican primrose. Mock orange, dogwood, lilac, pine, buddleia and quince are useful, easy-to-grow shrubs.

Protect your vegetables by constructing raised beds: these are easy to protect from birds as well as your dog with chicken wire covers; these can be covered later on with polythene or fleece to bring plants on earlier.

Burnt Lawns

Burnt lawns are more likely to occur with female dogs because they tend to empty their bladders in one go on the lawn, whereas males are more likely to urinate on surfaces other than the grass. It is the concentration of nitrogen in one spot that 'burns' lawns and other ornamental plants. One solution is to spray water over the place where your dog has just been. However, doing this could seriously damage your relationship with your dog if you do it every time he cocks his leg. So if you feel it's necessary, do it when he is not in the vicinity!

Some people add tomato juice or salt to the dog's diet, or even put baking soda into his drinking water: do not even consider these. They do not work and are extremely detrimental to your dog's health, leading to bladder disease or other painful illnesses. If that does not persuade you, then consider how much the vet's bills will be.

The only sensible solution is to take him for walks when he is likely to need to urinate, and to have a dedicated spot for him in your garden for when walks are out of the question. This does, however, require significant more training and effort, and it may well be more worthwhile to accept a few 'burns' in the grass.

9 EARLY DAYS

The first few days can be a stressful time for your dog, especially if he has been in the kennel environment for some time. This is not to say he will not enjoy being in a real home, but both positive and negative changes cause a degree of uncertainty, and your dog will be unsure what to expect from this new environment. Having a new owner is stressful in itself, and while many dogs seem to settle immediately, others take weeks or even months to be completely settled. Hopefully you will have arranged to have a few days, or even better, a week at home with your dog before having to leave him.

Nervous dogs may need time to learn to trust you, and may choose to spend time on their own. Don't worry if this happens, just ensure food and water are close to his preferred area and let him come to you. Fearful dogs need careful handling and their confidence can only be built gradually. With this in mind, there are some fundamental areas that you can influence to get both you and your dog off to the best start.

HOME COMING

The watchword is calm. All family members should keep their voices quiet and neutral; this applies especially to child members of the family. If your new dog's adrenalin levels are heightened by excitement, he will be unable to take in any of the early lessons you have planned. The best way to protect your dog from any additional stress is to set up a routine from day one and be consistent in your dog's training. This does not mean a harsh, inflexible timetable, but the result of decisions made by the whole family.

Just being in the company of a family should help to reduce your new dog's stress levels. In a 2006 study, one group of dogs were treated to human contact, which included grooming, petting and playing, for an average of 45 minutes each on their second day in the shelter. On the third day these dogs had much lower levels of cortisol (a stress hormone) than the dogs who had not received human contact[13].

It is worth remembering that smell is very important to your dog. Smells from air fresheners, incense, oils and perfume can confuse and stress him, particularly if they are, in his opinion, in great quantities. If you have ever been sickened by a particularly cloying perfume worn by another dinner guest or customer in a restaurant, then you will have some idea how distressing such unnatural smells can be for your dog. The message is, have a good sniff round yourself before you bring him home for the first time.

TOILET TRAINING

Ideally you should have a specific area in a direct route from one of your doors where your dog can go to the toilet. Using the same door every time will help him to associate going through this door with going to the toilet.

As soon as you bring your dog home from the re-homing centre, take him on the lead into the garden. If he manages to urinate, lavish him with praise. If he doesn't, take him back inside; give him some water and try again in about twenty minutes.

If you can be at home with your new dog for the first week, you will have more time to help reinforce his house training regime and to learn where his toilet area is located. Usually, dogs need to defecate after they eat. Canned food leads to more bowel movements than dry food, as the liquid content allows stools to pass more easily. High-fibre diets have the same result.

Dogs should urinate at least every eight to ten hours, depending on dietary factors such as the inclusion of sodium (salt) or glucose (sugar) and the amount of water consumed. The need to urinate will be greater during the day while he is active and drinking larger amounts. Also it is vital to remember that puppies, like babies, cannot hold themselves when they need to go to the toilet, therefore they must be taken out as often as you can.

If you are indoors when it is his usual time to relieve himself, take him on the lead to the designated place in the garden. If he doesn't manage to relieve himself in a couple of minutes, take him back inside and try again half an hour later. When he does manage to urinate, always remember to reward him. Be

It is natural for your dog to urinate frequently in outside spaces. He is marking his territory.

consistent in where you allow him to go: there is nothing more confusing than to allow him the freedom of the place one day only to restrict him the next.

Reinforce the idea by giving him his toilet command whenever you see him lift his leg, then move quickly towards his 'toilet area'. Eventually you will be able to tell him to go to the toilet and he will trot off by himself. However, if he has an 'accident' do not punish him. Ensure that you keep your eye on him, and if he shows any sniffing or circling towards a particular area quickly take him to the toilet.

Once you have decided where you want him to urinate, you could cover the area with pea shingle as dogs, understandably, like an absorbent surface. Avoid bark chips as these would absorb the urine, would be difficult to keep clean and would also smell. You could also hammer a post into the ground, which could be used in place of a tree. You need to keep this area as clean as possible, because dogs dislike an overflowing toilet as much as we do. This means you should regularly run the hose over the area and remove his faeces. You can bury them in the flower bed, put them wrapped in newspaper in the bin or even flush them down the toilet. But never put them on the compost heap as this may give any bugs in the faeces a chance to breed. Some people prefer to invest in a 'dog loo' which can be buried in the ground and chemicals added to treat the contents. However, this is not a 'green' method of disposal, and they can be too small for regular use.

DAY	ACTIVITY	BENEFITS
ONE	Start as you mean to go on and make it as easy as possible for your dog to get to know what he is supposed to do. Set the house training routine. Introduce him to the garden (on the lead). Praise and praise some more when he does something right!	By taking control and setting up a house training routine you may pre-empt any accidents.
	Introduce bed area and dogs items such as toys. Introduce food and drink stations and feeding routine. If you have another dog ensure that they are fed separately.	Introducing the areas which correspond with the all important maintenance behaviours (eating, drinking, sleeping and playing) is crucial to help him feel secure. If any one of these is absent it can lead to additional stress.
	Soon after you get home, take him for a short walk to stretch his legs. If it is late then the garden will be just as good. Do not take him to the local carnival! You will hopefully have many years to do that; you do not need to do it on the first day!	Taking your new dog for a short walk somewhere quiet is a good way to introduce him to his immediate area. It is important that his first trip out is as calm and relaxing as possible. His stress levels will already be raised, therefore if an event occurs which threatens him he is likely to be reactive and anxious and may learn something negative from the experience. Dogs can develop behaviour concerns with 'single event learning' which is the last thing you want on his first day.
	If you have another dog it is important to be watchful of both of them but also allow them to get to know each other and establish a natural order and behaviour. Use regular recall and breaks, especially if play is getting a little too intense. It is absolutely essential to feed them separately until they are used to each other.	Dogs in a multi-dog household should be allowed to find their own feet as they will be able to communicate and understand each other far better without our interference. However, a few management steps will help to reduce conflict and increase the probability of a good inter-canine relationship. Ensuring that play is kept 'cool' is one such technique.

	If you have a cat, keep her away from your new dog for a couple of days. But begin to introduce her gradually by placing something with her scent on it near to your dog's bed.	There is a great deal for him to take in on the first day and introducing your cat when stress levels are already high may result in mayhem. Allowing him to process your cat's scent and waiting until he is more settled should make her eventual appearance less arousing for him and more manageable for you. Remember: 'A stressed dog will find it very difficult to concentrate or take in and learn new information' and that is exactly what we need him to do when he meets the cat.	
	Allow your dog to have time out and rest without interference. If you have children ensure they leave him to settle. This day is all about letting your dog find his feet with a few pointers along the way. He may only want to sleep; if so, show him the basics and let him be. The same applies if he is nervous.	Allowing your dog to rest and take in all this new information at this early stage is paramount. He needs time to digest all the new experiences and this will not happen if he is over-stimulated. By allowing him to dictate the pace of the day, you will learn more about him. If he would rather sleep than play, let him but rouse him when it is time to eat as this is part of the routine you need to establish.	
TWO	Continue with the house training routine and continue to keep him on the lead in the garden.	It is important to continue your house training routine even if there have been no mistakes. If he has made a mess over night DO NOT PUNISH HIM. It will take time for him to settle. Remember he has been in a kennel where house training rules do not apply. If you punish him you are setting yourself up for some real problems in the future, not to mention it is a totally unreasonable thing to do.	
	Begin a loose exercise plan. Take him for a walk on the lead at the time you will normally be free to do so. Plan your route so that you avoid possible problems such as other dogs, noisy children or too much traffic. Choose areas that are more open so that you can put a distance between him and anything that may concern him. Repeat the same quiet route until you feel he is relaxed on his walks. Reward him when he is calm and confident and also when he focuses on you.	Using the same route each day is a great way to build his sense of security as he will know what to expect at each turn. By keeping him calm, you will be able to assess how he behaves when he is out and about. This will give you a measure of what is normal for him. These early days are about building trust and confidence between both of you. This is the only way your new dog can develop the all important secure attachment, the relationship and bond he has with you.	

THREE	Continue with the house training routine.	By continuing the routine you have the opportunity to learn his signals, in particular when he needs to go to the toilet. Do not worry if there are still mishaps as it really is early days.
	If he shows no sign of wanting to run away or hide while outside, increase his freedom out in the garden. Take some tasty treats if you are letting him off the lead altogether and give one to him each time he returns to you when you call him back.	If this is successful, it is a good sign that your dog is settling. Giving him treats for returning to you is all part of his training and the development of a good relationship with you. Don't spend too long on this as he may get bored or tired.
	If he is a nervous dog, continue to take him for walks along your original route. If he is confident, you may like to try a new route but look out for signs of stress.	The daily walk helps your dog to learn about the environment outside the safety of your garden. Monitoring his stress levels is important to ensure he remains within his comfort zone. This will also help you to get to know him and what concerns he may have.
	If your new dog is calm and able to concentrate it is time to introduce the cat. You will know he is ready for you to try when you are able to get his attention with vocals and reward.	This is a real test of your dog's personality. He may be indifferent, excited or alarmed – whatever the response keep the meeting short. A little and often is the way forward.
	Vet visit (register and health check).	Registering your dog with a vet ensures you are ready in case of any health emergencies. It is also a good idea to get a full health check as some of the smaller re-homing centres may not have been able to do this.
FOUR	Continue the house training routine. If you have an adult dog you may not need to take him out quite so often as at day two but it is still advisable to do so.	Taking him to the toilet area rather than waiting for him consolidates what he has learnt and avoids the possibility of accidents.
	Continue the cat introduction sessions.	Increase the sessions gradually to minimize stress.

Begin habitualizing your dog to being left alone. This is essential if you have taken some time off work and will be returning soon.

It is advisable to select an area of the house away from household items that you do not wish him to chew or even destroy, such as sofas. A good place for this could be either your hallway or kitchen. If they lead into each other you can keep your dog in one of them with a stair gate separating the two. This means your dog can still see what is going on but without access to anything he can damage.

Having decided on a safe area, furnish it with everything he needs: water, a soft place to sleep and a tasty treat which could be some of his dinner.

Leave him for a very short time – a few minutes at the most – before returning. When you go back in or let him out, do not make a fuss of him or ignore him. Just acknowledge he is there, possibly with a quick stroke, and carry on as before. Gradually increase the time you leave him while you are still in the house until you are confident he is settling without concern.

Leaving your dog on his own for gradually increasing lengths of time will habituate him to being alone. The main thing is to remain matter of fact about the whole procedure. Dogs are like children in that they can easily recognize your agitation and will respond accordingly. Although he may love your company, he will survive quite happily if left alone for short periods and the sooner he is trained to do this, the easier it is for him to accept this as part of his life with you.

Plan out the first few days of your dog's re-homing so you can establish that all-important routine.

INTRODUCING YOUR NEW DOG TO YOUR CAT

Dogs can be the best of friends with cats, however they must be correctly introduced for this to happen. Many dogs enjoy chasing other animals, and your cat is a potential target. Helping your dog to understand that your cat is not a 'chase object' is an important part of the introduction. It is equally important to help your dog remain confident and unafraid of the cat, as the traditional view of the dog chasing the cat is not always applicable.

If you have a cat, delay introducing her to your dog for a few days. It is a good idea to stroke her with a piece of material to collect her scent, and this can then be placed near to your dog's bed to familiarize him with his house mate. Keep the two separate until your dog has settled and become accustomed to his new home and the scent of his new companion.

Introductions in Practice

After a couple of days, when your dog has become accustomed to the basic routines of his new life in your home, you may feel the time is right to introduce your cat. Hopefully by this time your dog will know its smell, so is aware that your cat is a member of the household. The following are guidelines to a safe introduction:

- An hour after your dog has been fed is a good time to make the introduction, as his chase instinct will be dampened by his full stomach. Needless to say, both animals should be calm and contented.
- The cat should be in a high place, for example on a windowsill or the back of an armchair, with plenty of floor space for your dog so she does not feel threatened or crowded.
- Do not shut your cat in this area or force her to be there, as this will make her panic and become anxious. Use rewards and keep stroking her to encourage her to stay there.
- When the cat is settled, bring your dog into the room on a lead. Keep them as far as possible from each other, but so they are able to see each other. Present

Dogs and cats can be the best of friends.

the dog from a low level so that the cat feels secure. Do not block the entrance as this could lead to panic.

- Prevent your dog building up a 'stare', which is the behaviour that drives the chase instinct: do this by using the 'Watch me' command. When he is calm and quiet in the presence of the cat, give him a reward. You could use a clicker as long as you are confident in this technique (see Chapter 13).
- Keep the lead relaxed, and keep yourself calm and neutral. If the dog barks or becomes overexcited by the presence of the cat, this means that you are too close and you need to increase the distance between them. Do this if necessary, and reward your dog when he is calm once again. Do not punish him at any point.
- Conduct the introduction for five minutes to begin with, and increase the time gradually.
- Once your dog is consistently calm you can decrease the distance between the two animals, using positive reinforcement at each stage.
- When you feel that your dog is becoming habituated to your cat and is not demonstrating any desire to chase or harm her, you can lengthen the lead or use a long line (extra long lead), which gives you continued control while increasing his range. Use the 'watch me' command regularly, and conduct regular recalls. These will prevent him from getting into the 'chase sequence' and should be within your cat's tolerance level.
- When you feel confident enough to give your dog off-lead freedom in the same area as your cat, ensure you monitor the situation carefully. It can be very beneficial to put up stair gates that your cat can get through but the

dog cannot, so she can escape to separate areas of the house if threatened.

ESTABLISHING THE GROUND RULES

There are several factors that an owner must bear in mind when the rescue dog is settling in during the first few weeks. First, your new dog will not know what he is allowed or not allowed to do, especially if he has never lived in a house before, so it is important to be prepared to establish the 'rules' of the house on day one. This does not mean that you should reprimand him every time he contravenes your 'rules', but that you are ready with management techniques to modify your dog's behaviour sympathetically.

Out of Bounds

For example, when your dog arrives in his new home the first thing he will do is investigate his surroundings – at which point he may take a fancy to the best seat in the house, your sofa. This is particularly common in dogs that have had the full run of their previous home. However, it is not advisable to allow your new rescue dog to sit on the furniture. Firstly, it is unlikely that you will be so accommodating when he is covered in mud, and it is unfair to allow him access one day and deny it another. Being consistent also minimizes the chance of conflict: if you have never allowed him on the furniture, you will have no reason to nag him to get off.

Finally, a dog sitting on a sofa is closer to your face and head than a dog sitting on the floor, and you are therefore in a vulnerable position, defenceless against any aggressive displays if for any reason he becomes concerned – certainly a worthwhile consideration.

If you don't want your dog on the sofa, simply encourage him to the floor by offering him a toy or treat, and continue to reward him when he has got off it.

Positive Reinforcement

If your dog does sit on the furniture and you would like to get him off, do not tell him off or punish him: he may be simply investigating a new part of the house and has found a comfortable place to sit.

Avoid the common mistake of shouting 'down' and marching over to your dog to 'make' him move. What you are actually doing is backing him into a corner, and thus hemming him in. This is likely to frighten a new dog, as his only exit route is past the person aggressively shouting at him; consequently he may display defensive or even aggressive behaviour, as he is quite literally unable to escape.

Instead, use a treat or a toy to guide him off while you use the command words 'off you get' in a cheery voice. When he complies, positively reinforce this action with praise or the treat. Do not see this event as an opportunity to 'make' him know his place by aggression: it will damage your relationship, which in the early days may already be vulnerable.

If there are areas you don't want your dog to go, you can limit his explorations without constant vigilance or nagging by fitting a stair gate. This can be very useful, especially during the first few weeks.

'That's my dinner!'

Your dinner, drinks and snacks are all extremely tempting for your new rescue dog, and you must be aware that he may not know that your food items are out of bounds: monitor him around such items, and if he appears too interested, distract him and focus his attention away, rewarding him as you do so. A dog's sense of smell is so acute that he is able to detect food and drink from a great distance, and to him these items are highly desirable, even more than they may be to you!

It is better to establish certain management techniques so that the sound of smacking lips is not all that is left of the meal you worked so long and hard to produce. For example:

- Do not leave any food items on ledges or worktops.
- Do not leave food unattended at any time.
- Do not feed your dog from your dinner plate.

The first week needs careful planning, as this is when the ground rules are established. If you take the time and consideration to set up a suitable routine while being mindful of the areas that need extra preparation, you will have a solid foundation from which to progress. This will enable you to concentrate on settling your new friend into his home and building your relationship.

Items such as this glass can be a point of interest for your new rescue dog, especially if the contents are tasty.

10 AVOIDING MISUNDERSTANDINGS

Misunderstandings between dogs and their owners can cause disharmony within the relationship, and can have a significant impact on the owner's perception of the dog's behaviour. If an owner mistakes or misses an important signal – for example, fear of being stroked – the dog may be forced to increase its intensity, resulting in more misunderstanding. This is particularly damaging when forming a relationship with a dog already under the influence of stress and anxiety. The ability to understand your dog's signals will help you to gain his trust and to build his confidence in the relationship.

STRESS

A frequent source of misunderstanding, and subsequent failure in re-homing a rescue dog, is not recognizing that dogs can suffer from stress. While the kennel environment can evoke stress in dogs, this may be compounded by other circumstances, such as grief from the loss of their previous owner or existing stress levels due to abuse, whether intentional or misguided. Far too often this stress continues after adoption because many people do not understand canine behaviour and body language. Moreover, stress is not exclusive to dogs within the re-homing centre environment, and can be triggered by change of any kind, by the way the dog is handled, and by many other external stimuli.

People who suffer from panic attacks often experience the following symptoms:

- A rapid heartbeat
- Shaking, trembling and unsteadiness
- Hot flushes
- An urgent need to go to the toilet
- Not wanting to eat
- Frantic feelings and extreme emotions.

They may also experience many other

These two terrier-type dogs may be cross-bred individuals but the breed type they belong to has been specifically selected for farm work for generations.

upsetting 'feelings' and thoughts of dread. Now imagine a person on an aeroplane who is afraid of flying: as the plane takes off a panic attack is triggered and many of these feelings become a reality. Fortunately many people are able to rationalize the situation – unlike frightened dogs, which cannot do this.

Dogs experience anxiety when exposed to a fearful stimulus which they cannot rationalize, but where the threat remains the same: for example Sammy, a labrador female, whimpered when passing a dog she did not know, and her face contorted into deep furrows; Lady showed the whites of eyes and bared her teeth, and went and huddled in her bed, shaking, when anyone looked into her kennel; and Champ would spin round and round, jump up at his handler, trembling and with his mouth open, panting, when confronted by a stranger.

All these dogs were frightened, and reacting to stress in a recognizable manner. Some people believe their dog is just being 'silly' when they witness these behaviours. However, this reaction is easier than the alternative, which is to consider and review the circumstances that preceded this worrying behaviour. The point is that there is a reason behind every behaviour, and if the behaviour is concerning, it is necessary to question why it may be occurring to avoid a serious misunderstanding.

Stress is a psychological and physiolog-

The dog in the foreground is calm and relaxed, holding his ears loosely out to the side. His eyes are soft in appearance, without the sclera (white of eye) showing. His lips and mouth are also relaxed, and although he is panting because it is a hot day, his tongue is relaxed without tension.

ical response to a real or perceived threat to safety and security. When the stress response is triggered, the body prepares to run or fight, although it can equally become paralyzed with fear. A frightened dog can't explain his fear in words, but learning to understand him gives you control over the situation, and the ability to change things.

Stress Signals

The following behaviours are typical stress signals:

- Panting, not necessarily after exercise; the tongue is often held tensely out of the mouth and wider at the bottom)[14]
- Pacing
- Whining
- Barking
- Crying
- Inability to concentrate
- Facial ridges and furrows may appear

- Refusing treats
- Frantic behaviour
- Redirection-mouthing, nipping or biting their restraints.

BODY SHAKING

Many dogs display full body shaking to regulate their body after the influence of the stress hormone, adrenalin[15]. This regularly occurs after conflict with another dog, or when a nervous dog goes somewhere unpleasant, such as to the vet. Full body shakes can be the result of less specific causes. Reward any body shake with a simple 'good boy'. It is important to encourage the dog to do this because a body shake helps the dog 'get back to normal'.

The brown dog in the photograph is displaying 'mounting' behaviour towards the white terrier. Shortly afterwards the white terrier 'snapped'.

The 'snap', directed towards the brown dog, caused his adrenalin levels to rise sharply, leading to the full body shake. This is a stress-release mechanism.

COMMUNICATION

When we visit a foreign country we try to become familiar with the language spoken and the cultural customs. Most of us laugh at the story of the archetypal Englishman shouting to make himself understood; strange then, that so many of us shout commands to our dog when he appears unresponsive.

This is a ludicrous thing to do when you consider the superior hearing of the dog. A more reasonable approach would be to ask ourselves the following questions:

- Does he really understand what he is required to do?
- If so, are you asking him in the way he was trained to recognize?
- If you are, then he must be distracted. What is distracting him?

He may be distracted by something exciting that he wants to chase or play with. Alternatively, he may be in a state of heightened anxiety so that your message is not getting through. Continuing to shout will result in further stress, concern and potential anger in the dog, and the belief in the owner that his dog is disobedient, rude or dominant. However, helping him to overcome his stress will be mutually rewarding and a sign that you really do understand each other.

Culture

Do not fall into the trap of interpreting what your dog does in terms of human behaviour (anthropomorphism). Although dogs undoubtedly experience happiness, depression, fear and other less easily defined emotions, the situations that evoke these are quite different. We are revolted if we stand in a cow pat, whereas dogs adore rolling in them.

The blue merle collie is displaying potentially aggressive behaviour towards a dog walking past his kennel (out of this photograph). This could mislead potential owners into thinking he is a very aggressive dog, although he is not.

When we see a mouse, we may run in the opposite direction; when a dog sees a mouse, he sees prey and is genetically programmed to chase it. While most of the information about our environment is passed on via a mass of symbols such as speech, road signs, newspapers and television, dogs receive their information via their senses: sight, sound and smell. Their hearing and sense of smell are far superior to ours, although they are colour-blind to red and green.

Dogs evolved as hunters with a completely different perception of the world from our own. Their sense of smell is so acute that whereas we only see a bench, the way the bench smells is added to the dog's visual image. In other words, they literally 'smell the world', where we merely look at it.

The culture from which your dog originates is a group that must protect itself and its territory from outsiders. The individual members of the group must ensure that they get a share of the food, explaining why an insecure dog may guard his personal boundaries and his possessions. Another key feature of group behaviour is coordination: the behaviour of the group is totally synchronized so that they all eat, rest and hunt at the same time. This is a function of continued mutual observation, which means that every member of the group is at his peak level of energy when they hunt, and it allows them to work as a team.

Three lessons arise from these facts. The first is that, in the absence of his own species, a dog may become a little lost, therefore we must show him guidance. Secondly, he is programmed to use his skills to the benefit of the group. Dogs may not be as skilful as their wolf relatives in the wild at hunting, but attributes such as tracking, stalking, herding and many others have been selectively bred into the modern dog, so we can also benefit from them. Now that an increasing number of owners do not use their 'pet' working dog for these purposes, we can help our rescue dog to use these skills in games. Such games will stimulate and occupy him, and help him to bond with us.

Finally, dogs like us are social animals, and a dog left alone all day, without our attention or any focus, is a dog likely to suffer from such deprivation.

CANINE SOCIALIZATION

Canine Etiquette

Just as all cultures have a set of rules governing manners, so too do members of the canine family, and an ignorance of these rules can lead us to generate a great deal of anxiety which may lead to defensive or aggressive displays. Walks in the outside environment can be a social minefield for your dog. In the early days before he has become used to the route and the other dogs he may meet, you will help him enormously if you understand canine etiquette.

Left to his own devices, a well mannered, confident dog will often walk in a curve when approaching another dog, which is why many dogs may react strongly when they are forced to walk straight at someone. Allowing this preferred approach helps to keep your dog calm and confident. As the width of the curve depends on the individual dog, keep the lead loose so he can decide what feels right and safe for him.

It is considered particularly intrusive

The tan dog is placing her front paw high up on the other dog's shoulder. How a dog reacts to such a situation can depend entirely on the sex of the individual.

for an unfamiliar dog to rest his head or paws on another dog's back, as both of these signals can be viewed as either over-confident or threatening. Some dogs are more tolerant than others to this.

A polite dog negotiates with the other dog before approaching. This is carried out in ritual behaviour. First, potential hostility, aggression or friendliness is assessed from a few hundred metres away. At this point dogs decide whether or not they want to investigate further – well before they are able to meet nose to bottom. When they get close enough to make contact with each other they usually attempt to sniff each other's rear ends.

Dogs carry out this sniffing behaviour because it enables them to obtain additional information about each other – predominantly the sexual status. If the dogs are already friends they may bypass the bottom sniffing and begin playing straightaway.

Never force your dog to meet others. He may know best and may pick up signals of a threatening situation of which you may not be aware. Bear in mind that the lead can have an influence on the behaviour of your dog by making it more likely that he will be defensive because he is unable to run away from a threatening situation.

The Sign Language of Dogs

If we met a person who did not share a common language with us, then we would have to resort to the most primitive of gestures in order to communicate. Our dog, on the other hand, could communicate effectively with any dog, even one from the farthest reaches of the planet. Many people do not even realize that dogs also try to communicate with

The two dogs in this photograph are meeting for the first time. 'Bottom sniffing' is an important part of the greeting process, and owners should let their dogs carry out this behaviour.

us. But if our dogs are making this effort, then we should at least try to meet them halfway and be ready to interpret what they are trying to convey.

Below is a 'phrase book' of dog 'language' to help you to understand your dog. If you can understand and react accordingly to his behaviour, it will help relieve some of his insecurity about his new environment.

Dogs communicate with each other without words. Instead they use various body parts, postures and facial expressions, which may be emphasized by different vocal sounds. Most dogs have similar and repetitive signals that are easy for us to recognize. The re-homing centre will hopefully be able to tell you if the dog you are interested in has any idiosyncratic behaviour.

Odour also plays a part in dogs' recognition and interaction, although there is no need for us to get to grips with this aspect of communication!

Before studying the following signal list, you must bear in mind that it is important to look at the dog's whole body and to interpret his behaviour according to the situation. The same gesture may have different meanings in different contexts.

Being Afraid

The whole body may be lowered, and the dog's tail tucked between his legs to cover his scent. He may even freeze. The ears are usually laid back and tight against his head, and hair possibly raised along the back and shoulders (caused by adrenalin). He may also lick his nose, glance sideways and show the whites of his eyes (scelera). He may also show submissive behaviour such as rolling on his back. This situation needs handling carefully, possibly by removing the source of the fear, or him from it. A fearful dog may show potentially aggressive and defensive behaviours.

Aggressive Behaviour

The tail is often stiff and held straight up, and he may freeze. The ears seem alert, and he may stare directly into your eyes, or those of another dog. The hair down the spine and around the shoulders may be raised. The head and body may be lowered, or raised through posturing (dog to dog); the stance may be square; the foot pointing; hind legs ready to pounce and his attention focused. He may show his teeth or growl. A large percentage of aggressive behaviours stem from fear, therefore handle the fearful dog very carefully.

If you have any concerns with aggression you must make an appointment to see your vet and behaviourist, as this

Giles looks confident, with his head and tail held high, and body raised.

behaviour must be taken very seriously.

Alert

The tail is held high, the ears are erect and facing forwards. The alert dog is interested in what he looking at, thus it is desirable to encourage your dog to be alert towards you when training.

Calming Signals

Dogs use many signals to disarm a potential aggressor or to reassure each other. These signals include circling, lip licking, tongue flicks, yawning, sniffing the ground, looking away, moving very slowly and deliberately, and shaking the body as if shedding water. If your dog does any of these, he may be stressed or concerned, so you should try to work out why.

Dogs may also yawn when they want to be left alone or because they are tired,

Thelma is displaying a prominent tongue lick.

Dogs yawn when they are stressed by something in the environment. It can be something very simple, such as a person passing by a little too closely, or when they feel confused, or even when you are trying to photograph them, as is happening to Blue here.

which demonstrates the importance of context.

An understanding of these signals can help you to avoid misunderstandings. For example, if a person looks away when we are talking to them, we interpret this as disinterest or rudeness and mostly we would be right. However, if we are trying to communicate with our dog and he looks away or yawns, he is not being defiant, but is showing that he is very aware of your mood and it is making him anxious. Dogs may also sit down with their backs turned against you when you sound too angry. Don't make him even more concerned by shouting louder. This shows the danger of anthropomorphism: we should not interpret a dog's body language as you would a human's.

Turid Rugaas[16] suggests that you, too, can use these calming signals to reassure

The dog in the background is being stalked by the black dog in the foreground. Note how he is displaying several calming signals to pacify the situation, such as sniffing the ground without making eye contact.

your dog. If you are walking or playing and you notice a calming signal, then move slowly and look away. This should help to relax your dog. In other stressful situations, such as a vet visit or a busy gathering, you could try yawning or licking your lips. Dogs give their nose just a quick little lick when they are trying to calm each other, so there is no need to saturate yourself.

Greeting

Dogs lick others' faces and mouths when they greet one other to indicate friendliness. Briefly licking a person's hand after sniffing it is a form of greeting.

Happy

Tail wags are large and fast. The ears are relaxed and the hair will be smooth down the spine and shoulders. The dog might pant with relaxed lips, his movement is easy-going and fluid, and the eye contact soft without staring or glaring.

This dog is enjoying her time playing out of the kennel in the snow, and her relaxed body, face and tail, and the spring in her step, reveal this.

Hunting

When your dog is intent upon prey, he is under the control of powerful neuro-chemicals and is difficult to distract. As you may not want him to harm your neighbour's cat or even lay waste to the field mice population, it is useful to recognize the behaviour that indicates 'predator mode'.

When a dog begins a hunting sequence of actions he will scan his environment as he may have heard something that signifies 'prey'. When he locates it, he will look intensely in its direction. He may move very slowly towards it, but will then spring on to it suddenly. This sequence of behaviour can also be directed towards another dog and may be the prelude to play, or potentially to conflict.

If your dog becomes very still but focused, you should always be aware that this is the key behaviour in predation. Should this occur at an inappropriate moment you must try to distract your dog before he can complete the sequence.

Interest

There is a ridge above a dog's eyes, which serves the same purpose in communication as our eyebrows. When the 'eyebrows' are raised or the eyes are slitted, the dog is showing interest. He may also stamp his front feet while his back legs are still. Interest is also shown by holding the head high with the neck craning forward – although this could also mean that he is throwing down a challenge, so the context is important.

Playful

When your dog wants to play he displays what is known as the 'play bow'. In this he bows down and rests on his chest and front elbows, with his rear swinging

This collie is displaying a prominent 'play bow' towards the young pup. Note how the older dog is avoiding direct eye contact to show the pup not to be afraid, and to encourage her to play with him.

unconscious dependence on body language for verification. Therefore we are inclined to train our dogs purely through speech in spite of the fact that a dog's dominant mode of communication with other dogs is body language. Obviously, speech is necessary in calling your dog when he is busy sniffing around in the shrubbery. However, it is logical that movement should be incorporated in communication with our dog as a way of ensuring certainty and avoiding misunderstandings. In fact, we unwittingly communicate a great deal to our dogs through body language, such as placing our hands on our hips, pointing or smiling.

There can be problems with verbal communication, and this is why we feel that the whole family should sit down together and decide how they are going to communicate with their dog so some of these are avoided.

happily up in the air. After a short time, he may bark, run in circles, do a quick roll around, and return to the play bow. 'I will chase you and you can chase me' is what commonly follows this sequence.

Teaching Your Dog English

The old saying 'old dogs can't learn new tricks' is one that holds little truth. Dogs can learn new commands, behaviours and actions until they actually become senile. Therefore even a twelve-year-old rescue dog can be taught to understand your commands. Here we would like to suggest the most useful commands to teach your new dog. It is also important to remember that if your dog has received training in a previous home then you may need to learn what he knows. At this point you can begin re-educating your dog to respond to your commands.

As humans our dominant method of communication is speech, with a largely

Don't Go On About It

One mistake made by some dog owners – and indeed some parents – is that they just can't leave the message alone. Having said, 'Don't do that!' or 'Down!' they can't wait for the target of their message to respond. It is no wonder that neither dogs nor often children respond in these situations, as the original command has been over-ridden. To avoid falling into this trap you must train yourself to keep to the following rules.

There's no need to shout. Nobody wants an excitable, noisy, fearful dog or non-reactive companion. The way to prevent this occurring is for you to refrain from shouting and to keep calm. Remember that in a group the dogs watch and imitate each other and are receptive to such energy, so if you are using wide arm movements and a high-pitched voice, he is likely to do the dog equivalent and pick up on your actions.

Each 'sound' has one meaning: Whichever words you choose for your commands you must make sure that they are not duplicated. It doesn't matter what word you use, as long as both you and your dog know what it means.

How To Do It

- First get your dog's full attention by calling his name or saying, 'Watch me'. If he is concentrating on something else then he will not hear you. You can also use a treat as a lure to focus his attention.
- When he knows you are speaking to him, give your command and possibly accompany this with a hand sign.
- Give him a chance to respond.
- Don't forget to give rewards frequently (refer to Chapter 13 for essential clicker training), and never use physical force such as pushing him down. If he doesn't respond, don't be upset or angry, just repeat the command and show him what you want, for example pointing to, or patting the place you want him to be.
- Devise a different 'sound' and action for each of the following commands.

Sit: Teach the 'sit' command by using a treat to guide your dog's head and nose in an upward direction so that his bottom begins to touch the floor. Use the command you have chosen for 'sit', and as he sits, reward him. Be patient, as you may need to repeat this action several times if the dog is not familiar with the command; and remember to take regular breaks. When he begins to understand what to do you can introduce a hand signal, such as touching your shoulder with your opposite arm, and repeating the command.

Down: To teach the 'down' command, use a treat to guide your dog's head and nose towards the floor so that his head and body begin to lower. If your dog is stressed or anxious he may not want to lie down. Take things slowly: begin with asking him to sit, and gradually encourage him to relax and lie down. Use your command for 'down', and as he lies down, reward him. As he begins to understand what to do, you can introduce a possible hand signal, such as putting your hand behind your back, repeating the command.

Stand: To teach the 'stand' command, use a treat to guide your dog's head up, and take a step back so that he is encouraged to walk a step towards you in the stand position. As before, reward his success and later introduce a hand signal. Once the dog begins to understand the meaning behind your vocal or hand signals, you can reduce the 'luring', although you may need to return to it, especially if he becomes confused.

Stay: To teach the 'stay' command, begin with commanding him to sit. Then raise your hand and show your palm, and use the command 'stay'; wait a couple of seconds and reward him. Gradually build up the time and then the distance between you, always returning to him and rewarding him for remaining in the same place. It is important to move at his pace and increase the distance from him gradually. Reward him at each stage as you progress. If he gets up, don't worry, just go back to the previous step, repeating the command.

Wait: To teach the 'wait' command, stand

This dog's nose is being guided into a higher position, which automatically encourages him to sit down.

Once again the handler has lured the dog into the desired 'stand' position.

See how his nose has followed the handler's treat, so he has lowered his head to the floor.

The handler is walking behind the dog because he is performing an excellent stay command. This dog has been practising his training for some time, and it may take your dog a while before he can reach this stage.

up straight, use the hand palm up facing him, and ask him to wait. He can wait in 'sit' or 'down' or 'stand', that is up to you! If he begins to look distracted, repeat the command again to ensure he understands what he is supposed to do. 'Wait'

This dog is waiting patiently to be called and is focused on his handler.

is a prelude to the recall command, not the stay. Your dog will be expected to 'wait' and 'recall', rather than remaining still in one place.

Recall: To teach the 'recall' command, stand up straight and look at your dog as he waits, then smile, hold your arms out to the side, and call his name in a very enthusiastic way. As he reaches you, guide his head into the 'sit' as before, put two fingers in his collar and reward him, even if it has taken him a while to get back. This is important to ensure he does not move away after you have rewarded him if you need to put his lead on.

You can develop this association by ensuring that whenever your dog is near to you it is a positive experience. Use of punishment and harsh methods of training often results in dogs that do not want to go near their owners, let alone come to them when called.

It is clear to see that the dog is eager to reach his handler after being called. This is a vital part of the recall.

The handler's body language is clear and direct in this photograph. It is helpful to maintain open and positive facial and body postures all the way through the recall.

11 DOMINANCE, ATTACHMENT AND YOUR DOG

DOMINANCE HIERARCHIES: THE EVIDENCE

There is evidence that the domestic dog (*Canis Familiaris*) existed over 15,000 years ago. But in spite of the changes brought about by domestication, genetic analysis has shown that the domestic dog is an extremely close relative of the grey wolf (*Canis Lupus*), differing by at most 0.2 per cent of mtDNA sequence.

This is important to all dog owners, because fundamental views into canine behaviour and training stem from this information. However, our understanding of wolves is flawed, because most of our knowledge comes from research carried out on captive wolves. These are not necessarily related, but brought together from various sources and kept together for many years.

The term 'Alpha' when applied to any individual member of a species is associated with a dominance hierarchy. D.L. Mech[17] discovered that the classical dominance hierarchy previously recognized in captive wolf populations was actually different in wild wolf society. Far from establishing dominance through aggression, he claimed that dominance contests with other wolves are rare, and saw none throughout thirteen summers observing a pack in the wild. In real life the wolf pack is, in fact, a family that includes a breeding pair and their offspring, ranging from newborn to three years old. The offspring leave the pack once they are ready to mate.

Although the domestic dog is genetically very similar to the grey wolf, they are in fact very different. The domestic dog has a much smaller brain than the wolf,

and the behaviours of an adult domesticated dog – whining, barking and submissiveness – are found only in young wolves and not in adults. This is thought to have been caused by a process of developmental delay resulting in juvenile traits at maturity, and is known as neotony.

There is some evidence that these immature behaviours are the result of domestication. Since tameness and aggression are regulated by hormones, then selecting for tameness and against aggression could bring about a change to the physiological traits associated with domestication and neotony. In 1959, there was a breeding programme consisting of 100 female dogs and thirty male foxes[18]. Despite selecting only for tameness, many dog-like changes took place in the foxes: skulls became wider and snouts became shorter. There were also individuals with floppy ears, shortened tails, curly tails and piebald coats. As the study continued throughout the twentieth and into the twenty-first century, the farm foxes also showed signs of a change in the reproductive cycle, with biannual oestrus, a feature occurring in the domestic dog and not in wolves.

This research was used to support a later theory[19] that dogs did not evolve directly from wolves; instead they domesticated themselves to exploit a new ecological niche, Mesolithic village dumps. It is from these wild village dogs that researchers believe the domestic dog was selected. Arguing that no one has ever successfully trained a wolf, they suggest these village dogs would be more

The word 'dominance', and in particular the phrase 'dominant dog', has created a divide among the professionals, with two 'camps' for and against the principle of the dominance hierarchy existing between dogs and their owners. A dominance hierarchy classically refers to the organization of a group of animals of the same species, and concerns the control and circulation of resources within a territory. Higher-ranking individuals gain control through a dominance contest that gives them the right to obtain the resources such as food and mating rights above other members of the group. This in turn enables them to achieve reproductive superiority.

docile and easily trained to do whatever jobs we wanted them to do.

Neotony in dogs suggests that mentally they are at the stage of the adolescent wolf or the wolf cub, and are not psychologically prepared to take on the responsibilities of a pack. Therefore the idea that they need a parental figure rather than an authoritarian leader becomes more appropriate and realistic.

Other researchers[20,21] also discovered that domesticated dogs, which are free to roam the streets, do not form packs with dominance hierarchies. Domesticated dogs no longer need to form large packs to hunt prey because they have humans to supply food for them.

Finally, a dominance hierarchy typically refers to a group of animals of the same species. Therefore we must question the possibility of a hierarchy consisting of two distinct species. To suggest they view humans exactly as 'other dogs' seems a complete over-simplification.

Our 'juvenile wolf', the dog, lacks the maturity to take responsibility and leadership of the pack, is unlikely to regard humans as other dogs, and has no need to control resources. All this suggests that some, if not all, so-called 'dominant behaviour' is the result of another psychological process.

The adult pointer in the centre of this photograph is displaying submissive body language because he feels threatened by the older dogs. The older dogs did not show any potentially aggressive behaviour towards him; his behaviour stems from his lack of confidence. Although many adult dogs behave in such a way when threatened, it is not so apparent among adult wolves.

THE TWO 'CAMPS'

There are those who favour the idea that our domestic dog is likely to initiate a 'dominance contest' with us. They believe that you must pre-empt any such attempt by showing your new dog that you are in charge, and that he is at the bottom of your 'pack'; they stress that you must suppress any 'dominant behaviour' and 'show him who is boss' to make certain that he does not threaten your superiority. Failing to establish this will lead to a 'dominant dog' who believes he is the pack leader and will consequently ignore your commands and generally do as he pleases.

On the other side are those who believe that dominance hierarchies do not exist between owners and their dogs in the way previously understood, and that the behaviour commonly perceived as 'dominant', is the result of a different psychological process. In this view attempts to reduce a dog's 'status' are not only unnecessary and confusing for the dog, but can be detrimental to the overall relationship. They believe that you can live harmoniously with your dog using training and guidance without the constant pressure of asserting your dominance over him. The aim of this chapter is to enable you to question whether or not branding your dog as dominant is fair, useful and, most importantly, conducive to a successful re-homing.

An Alternative Hypothesis

The concept of the dominant dog sits uncomfortably with many of us, because many so-called 'dominant' behaviours could be caused by many other factors, in particular by a dog's insecurity and fear. Moreover, these emotions will increase in intensity when threatened with further conflict and stress. It is therefore possible that an animal under stress, confused and with a disruption in his core needs, may demonstrate what was classically known as 'dominant' behaviour, which in reality is a by-product of his emotional state, over which humans have direct influence.

When a dog tries to go through a door before you, he may not be asserting his superiority, but is merely eager to see what's on the other side. When your dog jumps on the sofa, it may be that he is not purposefully requisitioning the seat with the highest status, but has simply found a comfortable place to sit. When your dog growls at you because you rush across the room, shouting with hands grabbing, about to pull him off the sofa, it may be that he feels threatened and is fearful of these actions – so his display of defensive behaviour to your aggressive body language may have very little to do with dominance. Similarly, dogs who growl at owners who try to remove the food bowl half way through eating may simply be hungry rather than dominant – in the most extreme cases this is a direct threat to survival itself.

This is not to suggest that any of these behaviours is desirable or acceptable; however, dogs are complex mammals with a survival drive not dissimilar to our own. They have the ability to feel emotions, including stress and fear, and the ability to recognize when they need to display threatening behaviours. In view of this, we should be sympathetic to their response to perceived threats, and make an effort to understand when they are feeling this way.

If we substitute the adjective 'dominant' with 'survival' as in 'survival behaviour', then we realize that there is something very wrong in a relationship where a dog is showing any 'survival

Jumping up for a cuddle does not necessarily mean your dog is trying to dominate you; he may just want to get as close as he can to say 'hello'.

behaviour', especially towards a human. This in turn makes us question what could be wrong, leading us to speculate that it could be fear of a phantom in the shape of a 'dominant dog'.

The Implications for Your Dog

At this point you may be thinking, 'So what? Surely, it's just a difference in terminology?' The problem is that this terminology often has a direct impact on the treatment the dog receives. When people believe that their dog is challenging their status they are often very quick to do all they can to reduce him to a submissive role. At its mildest, attempts to reduce 'dominance' are limited to

obedience and control, for example training your dog to walk through a door behind you, rather than pulling you through it, or walking close to your heel. Both camps teach these rules because they are beneficial from a safety and practical point of view, but for one group they are regarded as a means of asserting authority. In more extreme attempts the dominant dog may be 'forced' to be submissive and subservient through the use of punishment. This is despite the possibility that his behaviour may not be motivated by status.

The rationale behind punishment is that it is used in the wild and is therefore appropriate in a domestic setting. The use of punishment arises from the belief that the Alpha male in a wolf pack is prepared to establish and enforce his authority by inflicting pain on his subordinates. Regardless of whether or not you believe your dog is trying to dominate you, using training methods that

THE ORIGIN OF SUBMISSION

In wolves, behaviours such as dominance and submission are developed during the period when the mother wolf starts the process of reducing her cub's dependence on her. In response to the mother's snapping, growling or nipping, the cubs will lie on their backs in a posture we describe as 'submission'. This posture can also be seen in our domesticated dogs, and the general belief is that it is in response to a dominance gesture. However, the pup is not afraid of the mother, but is showing that he knows he has displeased her and is prepared to change his behaviour. If we view dominance–submission from the perspective of parental care, we see that our neotonized dog perhaps views us as a guardian responsible for his welfare and behaviour, rather than as a pack leader whose position he needs to challenge.

evoke pain and suffering should be avoided at all costs.

In the absence of definitive proof that cross-species hierarchies exist, the hypothesis that so-called 'dominant behaviour' can be the result of other processes is very compelling.

A Training Perspective

Not only do we have a moral obligation as an intelligent higher species to avoid inflicting pain and suffering on any living creature, but the consequences of such actions can cause a considerable number of behaviour concerns as well. Very worryingly, punishment leads to fear, and fear is the source of many behaviour concerns, including aggression. It can produce a very insecure or defensive individual and, ironically, can lead to further 'survival behaviour'.

Training using punishment is not only unfair and unreasonable, but may be dangerous and destructive. Furthermore, you can achieve the same outcomes without having to use such methods, as we will explore in Chapters 13 and 14.

Our reasoning is not based exclusively upon taking the 'moral high ground', as we believe it is in everybody's best interest to think about the impact of their own behaviour on their dog, and to consider the effects of specific training. Before we delve deeper into this important discussion we must introduce the concept of attachment status. This will help you to understand the importance of your actions and how they are inexplicitly linked to your dog's overall behaviour and welfare. It should also help to show why every owner should 'care' about how they are influencing their dog's behaviour, especially when contemplating the use of punishment.

ATTACHMENTS

Attachment can be simply understood as the bond and the relationship you have with your dog. Although attachment was first used to explain the bond of affection that develops between a human infant and its caregiver, it has since been recognized as applicable to many social species, including dogs.

Laboratory tests have found that the dog's relationship to humans seems similar to a child-parent relationship. This is because the behaviours demonstrated in the test situations can be categorized along the secure-insecure attached dimensions, as in human mother-infant interactions[22]. A secure attachment is essential for a baby to develop into a psychologically healthy adult, and there are also important implications for dogs. The level of attachment your dog has with you and other members of your family can be directly influenced by what he has experienced in the past, and what

This labrador is enjoying a scratch on the rump. He has a secure attachment status, and is happy to have close contact with people, even those he does not know very well.

he experiences in the future.

There are four categories of attachment. A dog with a secure attachment status is happy to have close contact with people, even those he does not know very well. A dog with an avoidant attachment may be reluctant to approach, let alone be handled. The attachment you have with your dog is a very important aspect of understanding why he behaves in a particular way.

Dogs that have a secure attachment status are likely to be those who express mostly favourable behaviour; dogs that have an insecure attachment vary in three ways, but generally do not like

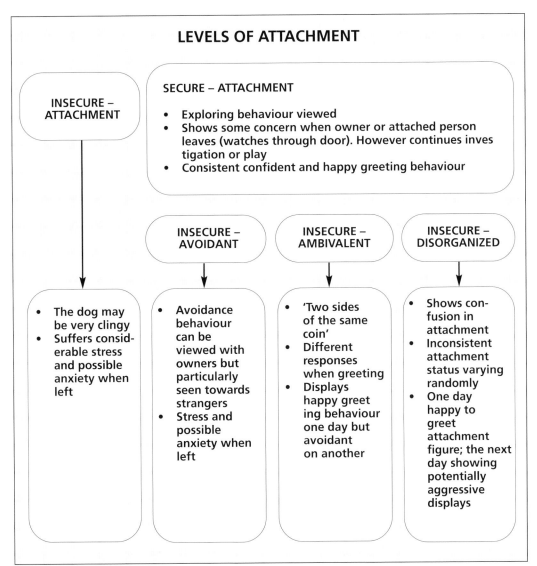

LEVELS OF ATTACHMENT

INSECURE – ATTACHMENT

SECURE – ATTACHMENT

- **Exploring behaviour viewed**
- **Shows some concern when owner or attached person leaves (watches through door). However continues investigation or play**
- **Consistent confident and happy greeting behaviour**

INSECURE – AVOIDANT

INSECURE – AMBIVALENT

INSECURE – DISORGANIZED

- The dog may be very clingy
- Suffers considerable stress and possible anxiety when left

- Avoidance behaviour can be viewed with owners but particularly seen towards strangers
- Stress and possible anxiety when left

- 'Two sides of the same coin'
- Different responses when greeting
- Displays happy greeting behaviour one day but avoidant on another

- Shows confusion in attachment
- Inconsistent attachment status varying randomly
- One day happy to greet attachment figure; the next day showing potentially aggressive displays

When a dog has a secure attachment he is happy to be with you and secure enough to show some independence.

being left alone, are 'clingy' and 'needy', and may show other concerning behaviour. Thus an insecure avoidant dog may choose to avoid human contact altogether and may be very reluctant to approach you; an insecure ambivalent dog will show varying degrees of greeting behaviour, at times friendly and affectionate, but can show defensive behaviours alongside these greetings. An insecure disorganized dog shows random greeting behaviour of extremes, and can be of real concern.

INFLUENCING A DOG'S BEHAVIOUR

Building a dog's attachment status and security requires the development of trust through positive experiences. Punishment is a negative experience, and consequently very likely to undermine the attachment between you and your dog.

When a dog is displaying undesirable behaviour it may well be due to lack of direction through training, or because there is a disturbance in any of its maintenance behaviours (core needs). This brings us to an examination of the specific techniques used to influence a dog's behaviour. Positive reinforcement means the dog is rewarded when he carries out a behaviour you want, and this results in the dog's brain releasing feel-good chemicals, making him very likely to enjoy training and to learn progressively.

The only thing that punishment produces is fear. Therefore we advise you not to use any of the following training methods.

Electronic collar: This device enables a trainer to deliver electric shocks of varying strength by remote control. It uses extreme punishment to inflict pain when a dog displays a specific behaviour. Just imagine the fear and confusion of the dog, unaware that a device has been strapped to his neck but more than aware of the pain when his behaviour results in electrocution. This is a sure way to traumatize your dog, create depressive emotions and lead to total shut-down of the mind.

Vanessa worked with a dog so traumatized by having been 'trained' in this manner that she could not be in the same room as any item that reminded her of the device. She would shake and tremble at the sight of a remote control, and became noise phobic to the point that she found the outside world almost unbearable. Just imagine how this affected her attachment status, trust and confidence in people. This little collie was deeply affected and it took years for her to begin to trust again.

Spray collar: This device emits a mist spray often into the dog's face which can be activated by remote control or set off by vibrations such as barking. These devices can also cause the dog to become shut down and depressed through suppression of behaviour, and can also cause phobic reactions to noise.

Throw chain: This is thrown at the dog's rump when he is doing something you don't like, or even to attract his attention. Imagine the pain if you hit him with too much force or in a vulnerable place such as the eye.

Shake can filled with pebbles or coins: Such items are used to shake at the dog to startle him so that he stops what he is doing. Again, these contribute to the dog's concerns, and in addition do not tackle the emotional components of the behaviour.

Squirt bottle or squirt gun: These are filled with water with maybe a small amount of mouthwash or vinegar mixed in so it is more of a deterrent. This can suppress the unwanted behaviour, but can cause a phobic reaction to water and a very anxious dog.

'Flooding': This expression describes over-loading the dog with something he is concerned about; it can also be extremely detrimental. For example, a dog that is afraid of other dogs is made to sit in a room full of them. This can lead to total withdrawal for those unfortunate dogs unable to escape from the situation, especially if punishment is used as well. The dog is likely to get a great deal worse in his concern, or reach a point of such anxiety and stress that he starts to shut down. This should be avoided.

Choke chain devices: These cause pain and a tightening impact when the dog pulls. Although still widely used, they are not advisable as they can even cause injury when used incorrectly.

Traps: Booby traps are set so that if a dog steals food or raids bins something falls on him and causes him to experience pain or become fearful. This could lead to severe anxiety and insecurity.

Ironically these methods merely suppress the target behaviour, as the cause of the concern has not been taken into consid-eration. Suppressing unwanted behav-iours may lead to 'spontaneous recovery', when the behaviour will come back much worse in the future or cause it to reccur in a different manner. You cannot help a dog overcome his concerns by electrocut-ing him: you will simply make things a great deal worse, and cause him to suffer along the way.

Only by tackling the reason why your dog is behaving in a specific way can you modify his behaviour and shape it into a different response. If you electrocute or shake a can of stones at a dog that barks and growls at other dogs through fear, it does not stop him experiencing the fear emotion. It does not make him feel more confident, less afraid and more likely to be sociable. It just suppresses the barking or growling so that it does not show any more, but he is still afraid, and the reason why he is behaving in this manner has been overlooked. This is the fundamental problem with using punishment and to a degree negative reinforcement.

The alternative to causing pain and suffering is to tackle a concern. The inter-esting thing is that the alternative is often easier and more effective than you think.

The dogs in this photograph are young and boisterous and are engaged in a rough play session. They are able to enjoy such play because they are all confident and well-socialized individuals.

SUCCESSFULLY TRAINING THE RESCUE DOG

Throughout the book we reinforce the importance of training, guidance, and direction in your dog's life; showing owners how to engage the natural dog to become content and a pleasure to live with. This is supported by our desire to make such training a success for everyone, with a particular focus on the rescue dog and his owner, who may need a little more help to accomplish this.

Training with punishment through fear can lead to further aberrant behaviour resulting from heightened levels of anxiety. The rescue dog by definition may already have suffered in some way and his attachment status may be fragile.

One thing is certain, if you want to successfully re-home a rescue dog, this will not happen if you are ignorant of the kinder and fairer ways to influence your dog's behaviour.

CASE STUDY

Benny is a four-year-old lurcher cross male who was re-homed from a rescue organization two years ago. When Benny's owners first took him home they had a few settling in problems, with Benny nipping them on two occasions. The first time was when his owners held Benny by the collar to move him off the sofa, and the other when they pushed him down for jumping up excitedly. From the time he was brought home, Benny showed fear-related concerns towards being handled, and considerable fear at the sight of items such as belts and brooms.

Benny showed an insecure ambivalent attachment with his owners to begin with, but this changed to become much more secure over time. Once he settled in, he became one of the family and his owners had no further concerns.

However, after two years problems began when Benny was out for his walks. He began to show aggressive behaviours towards other dogs when on and off the lead. His owners punished him for this, and he began to get worse. In the home Benny's behaviour also changed, and he started to show an insecure ambivalent attachment once again. He began to growl at his owners when they attempted to stroke him, and one time even bit the male owner on the hand. Benny received punishment for these behaviours and began to withdraw into himself. He stopped playing with his toys and was increasingly inconsistent in his greeting behaviour.

At this point his owners felt that something must be done or they would have to return him to the re-homing centre.

The first step was to identify what was going wrong in the relationship, and why Benny was behaving in this manner. He had a history of being fearful, and he came in the category of ambivalent attachment before his owners had gained his trust. This trust, however, started to break down through the use of punishment and then Benny's ambivalence reappeared. Understandably, he was also becoming very miserable and not at all himself.

His owners took a step back from the situation and contacted Vanessa. Under her instruction they began the first phase of helping Benny to rebuild his security, and stopped the punishment. The second phase involved building trust through positive reinforcement. Almost at once each of Benny's concerns began to disappear and within two weeks he started playing with his toys again. However, it took him several months to develop the confidence and security he needed to become more securely attached and confident.

This story demonstrates the importance of attachment in dogs, especially in the case of the rescue dog that may already have been through upheaval and inconsistency.

12 THE IMPORTANCE OF SOCIALIZATION

Socialization is the process by which the dog learns to accept and communicate with other dogs. In the wild he learns this by observation. The domestic dog learns from birth with his litter-mates and mother how to interact with other dogs. However, when he is taken from the litter and placed in a home it is vital to continue his education throughout his life.

Socialization is beneficial for the dog as dogs are a social species, and interaction with others enables them to relieve stress and excess energy as well as generally enjoy themselves. As dogs learn effectively from observing each other, socialization can also encourage learning of other important behaviour as well as canine social skills. Thus a well-socialized dog will be able to cope with meeting other dogs and will know precisely what to do. This can make it much easier for an owner, especially when it comes to walking, on and off the lead.

The first part of this chapter uses illustrations to show the variety of canine interactions and scenarios that you may encounter on a daily basis. We then examine the many causes of breakdown in social behaviour, and look at how you can help your dog to become a sociable individual.

STAGES OF OFF-LEAD SOCIALIZATION

Meet and Greet

Meeting and greeting is all about finding out information about each other. If a dog lacks confidence he is much more likely to show nervous, defensive or potentially aggressive behaviours. This is why it is important to encourage dogs to remain calm and relaxed when greeting each other.

It is important to remember that when a dog gives the 'hair raising' signal, this does not necessarily mean that he is going to display aggressive behaviour. It could just as likely signify that he is a little nervous and will move away. Thelma, the black and tan dog in the photograph overleaf, is not making direct eye contact and she is showing the beginning of a paw lift, both of which are signs that she may be attempting to diffuse the tension during this 'meet and greet' phase.

Ben, the blue merle collie in the picture overleaf, is displaying some nervous behaviour in his reclined stance, as he is ready to move away quickly if necessary. He shows tension in his face, his mouth is tight, and he appears uncertain.

At this stage in the 'introduction', dogs assess the other dogs and process the information to decide if they want to continue the interaction. If they do not want to make friends, the situation may

These three terriers have just met for the first time, as can be seen in their 'posturing' body language. Each is standing square, head high and tail straight up.

Thelma (black and tan) and Ben (blue merle collie) are displaying revealing body language. Thelma's increased adrenaline levels are evident by the raise of her hackles.

The white terrier in the foreground is looking away in an attempt to diffuse any potential conflict.

become increasingly tense, with growling, circling, or increasing posturing with no lapse. If this occurs, it is advisable to move them on. Do not touch them or get in between them. Instead use a command such as 'This way', in a cheery, strong voice, to encourage a break in behaviour. In addition use a toy such as a ball to encourage them to lose focus on the other dog.

Above all avoid adding to the tension by telling the dogs off, because this is likely to make matters worse.

The Play

This is often the fun part. Many dogs absolutely love to play and chase one another, and it is highly beneficial for them to participate in this stage of the socialization process.

These three dogs are off for a fast play session. After some brief posturing and introductions, it is now time for the fun.

Herding

Dogs that become very focused on herding behaviour, and which tend to get rather carried away, need to have regular 'time out' sessions. This can be achieved by calling the dog back to you and asking him to do something else. This will slow his heart rate and reduce his adrenalin levels. If he begins to show any nipping behaviour, ask him to focus on you, or issue some simple commands such as 'sit' or 'paw', or even give him some brief time on the lead.

Herding behaviour is precisely what collies are bred to do and is very much part of their make-up. Helping them to focus this energy away from potential targets can be useful, but you may find that this is very typical of how they play. This is not necessarily a negative thing, it just needs to be monitored.

When Things Get Too Much

Many dogs play very roughly with each other, and the rough and tumble of a canine play game can be quite alarming. This is absolutely normal and many dogs love playing this way. Other, more sensitive dogs, or very young or older individuals, may not be so keen to join in, and they can become quite concerned by such behaviours. Therefore you should keep an eye on your dog for any sign of distress or anxiety, or that he has had enough and is ready to continue the walk alone.

Ignoring such signals can be detrimental to your dog and can cause future concerns, especially if he is forced to show aggressive displays to reinforce how he is feeling. While it is quite normal for dogs to 'tell each other off' with a warning growl, care needs to be taken if this escalates or one of the dogs is not

Toys can be a source of conflict between dogs, so it is a good idea to remove any toys when dogs of uncertain character are playing freely.

Things can get a little too much for some dogs, and the cocker spaniel is displaying submissive behaviour in response to meeting the three other dogs in this photograph.

responding to these warnings. Mostly dogs are far better than we are at diffusing such situations, but forewarned is forearmed, so be prepared to intervene by re-directing their attention.

Many younger dogs display submissive behaviour to show that they are not a threat. As they grow in confidence and are socialized with less threatening individuals they are likely to show less of this behaviour.

POTENTIAL CONCERNS WITH SOCIALIZATION

Concerns with socialization are common among owners, as the new environment may heighten the existing stress in the newly re-homed dog. This can lead to increased fearfulness and therefore defensive behaviour towards other dogs,

even in a dog that is normally happily sociable. This section will guide you through what is needed to help your rescue dog remain a well-socialized individual.

The Impact of the Lead

Do not underestimate the influence of the lead. The lead is a vital piece of equipment for all dog owners as it keeps the dog safer than he would be without constraint, and it greatly increases the range of locations you can take him. Having the dog on a lead can, however, cause a difference to behaviour. The tension on the lead is the primary cause of this change as it creates a psychological response in the form of stress, frustration and anxiety. This is because the dog is restricted so that he is unable to express his natural behaviour. The lead can influence how the dog stands, walks and manoeuvres, particularly when he pulls against it.

Try to visualize a dog on a lead and a playful collie off the lead bounding up to him. The dog on the lead is excited and pulls a little as he is eager to approach. The lead causes the neck and chest to rise up and the dog instantly begins to tense under this constraint. When he pulls even harder, his front paws lift from the ground so he is standing on two legs. Some dogs may not understand that these movements are due to the influence of a lead, but feel they are under threat. Added to this is the frustration of not being able to greet the collie, along with the fact that he cannot run away should he need to. This situation is rife with misunderstandings for both the dog and owner, who may mistake the pulling and barking for inappropriate behaviour.

The lead has an impact on a dog's posture when he pulls against it, and this can have an effect on the way other dogs perceive him because his body language is altered.

The Key to Success

You can still achieve successful introductions and interactions while your dog is on the lead; just keep as relaxed as possible and allow the dog to express his natural behaviour while remaining under control. The following points aim to help you to achieve this.

- Be aware that your hand is directly controlling your dog's neck or body (if on a harness), and the way you handle the lead, will affect the way he is feeling. Don't be a 'dead weight' on the handle or tug against the dog, as this will lead to him pulling against you, resulting in tension, stress and potential anxiety. You will, in fact, make it more difficult for your dog to resist you if you gently guide him with the lead.
- Tension needs to be kept to a minimum because it is this force that can create the concern. If a dog feels relaxed, happy and confident he is much more likely to reflect this in his body language as he greets his fellow dogs. Equally, tension, frustration and stress are also likely to be transmitted during an interaction, and to lead to defensive behaviour.
- Allow your dog to say 'hello' and sniff potential friends, as long as he is not displaying any potentially aggressive behaviour. He may be excited, which is normally signified by high-pitched whines and rapid wags of the tail. In this case you should remain calm, focus his attention and allow him to express his natural greeting. If he becomes over-excited you can circle him away to gain a little more distance, but for many dogs once they have got to their play friend the vocals stop as quickly as they began!

- Allowing your dog to say 'hello' also avoids him building up feelings of frustration, but the situation and the dogs' characters need to be established before you can let your dog move close to another. It is always advisable to call to the owner of the unfamiliar dog before such encounters occur to ask them if their dog is friendly. Do not blindly follow this, however, and be constantly aware of how both dogs are behaving.
- If your dog has a history of aggressive behaviour towards other dogs it is essential to seek the advice of your vet and behaviourist.

Training Classes

Training classes or supervised group walks can be a fantastic way to teach your dog how to interact with other dogs in a supervised manner. Ask your re-homing centre for recommended trainers and classes. Dogs will also benefit from mixing with different people in this environment: a further aspect of socialization for the domestic dog is to teach him to accept humans and human situations in a positive and acceptable manner. The aim is to be able to take your dog to any place or situation, and for him to stay calm, relaxed and confident. A poorly socialized dog is unpredictable when placed in a new or frightening situation. In such situations he may become over-excited, anxious or very active.

Before you attend a class, make certain that your dog will not be too fearful of, or have any concerns with this environment. A class situation can exacerbate the behaviours of some dogs by 'flooding' them with their major concern, such as too much noise or too many strange dogs. If this is the case, he will need to attend specialist sessions otherwise his concerns will become more serious.

WHY TRAINING CLASSES CAN BE SO BENEFICIAL

- You can learn how to communicate effectively with your dog, discover what he knows and strengthen your relationship together. Many rescue dogs have already undergone some training before re-homing, and classes can be a pleasurable way of discovering what he can do. You may be pleasantly surprised and find yourself at the top of the class with your rescue dog!
- You and your dog can learn new commands and behaviour, to develop the abilities of you both and to encourage your dog to behave in a desirable way.
- Although many classes focus on training commands and not specifically 'off lead' socialization, they often cover 'loose lead' walking and recall while in a group environment. However, there are other groups that focus on socialization, in particular those involving supervised walks.
- Each dog arriving for training will be accompanied by at least one person, sometimes more. This means the class is an excellent and safe place to build your dog's confidence around lots of people, as it takes place in a controlled environment.
- Training classes are fun! Many dogs and their owners absolutely love going to classes, using their brains and meeting new friends. Your dog will receive mental and physical exercise when attending training classes.
- Through classes you may discover at what type of activity your dog excels. This could give you an insight into further activities in which you and your dog can participate: agility, obedience and heelwork to music are just a few of the activities you can get involved in, and have great fun in the process.

13 A STITCH IN TIME

INVESTIGATING BEHAVIOUR CONCERNS

We firmly believe that language influences thought, so throughout this book we have substituted 'problem' with 'concern', and 'bad behaviour' with 'undesirable behaviour'. We hope that this alone may influence how you view a behaviour concern, and if so, that it will contribute to your successfully re-homing a rescue dog.

So what is bad behaviour? Bad or naughty behaviour can be anything that 'we' choose to label as such: usually it is undesirable, inconvenient, embarrassing or potentially hazardous. The problem with this label is that it is often linked to punishment varying in severity according to the person carrying it out. This approach is fundamentally flawed, as behaviour is only 'bad' or 'naughty' if the perpetrator is aware that this is a transgression. In our view, this is an extreme case of anthropomorphism, as we would argue that dogs do not have the cognitive ability for such duplicity. The case study of Jake offers a better insight into this proposition.

Shaping Your New Dog's Behaviour

From the very beginning of the re-homing process, remember that life has changed dramatically for your new dog. It may, therefore, take him time to settle and for you to get to know him. He will

CASE STUDY: JAKE
'BAD' IS IN THE MIND OF THE BEHOLDER

Jake was a six-year-old neutered black labrador-cross male; a year after coming to the re-homing centre he was adopted by a very kind and capable couple along with another dog.

Several weeks later his owners contacted the centre with news that Jake was displaying the potentially aggressive behaviour towards people out on his walks that he had earlier overcome. During Vanessa's meeting with them, a very important point arose: Jake's owner asked how Jake would understand that he was behaving badly if he was not told off. In other words, how would he distinguish between acceptable and unacceptable behaviour if it were not marked by a negative response?

This is a very important question, and one that has a great bearing on how to approach training in general. Jake's behaviour was 'bad' for his owners for all the reasons we first mentioned. Jake, however, was not being purposely bad or naughty, but was merely responding in a normal and logical way to the emotion he was feeling. In this case, the emotion was fear and his behaviour reflected this. Clearly the solution was not punishment, as this would only have contributed to his concerns or suppressed the behaviour without dealing with the cause.

Vanessa's recommendation was to focus on shaping the way Jake was feeling to help him to overcome his concerns about strangers.

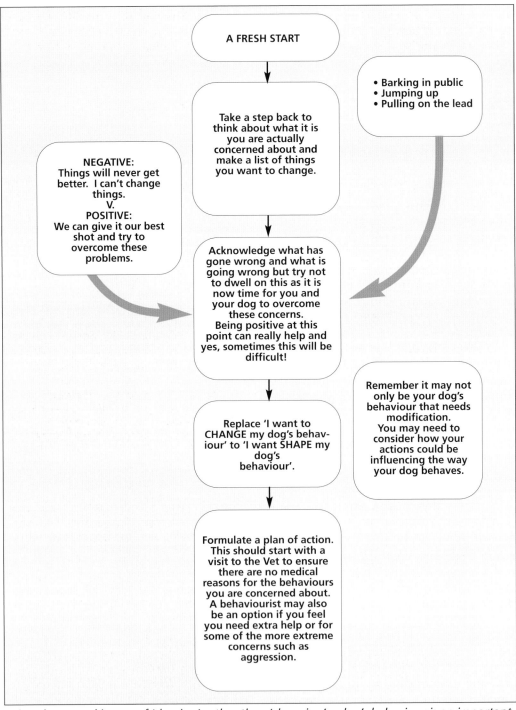

A FRESH START

- Barking in public
- Jumping up
- Pulling on the lead

Take a step back to think about what it is you are actually concerned about and make a list of things you want to change.

NEGATIVE:
Things will never get better. I can't change things.
V.
POSITIVE:
We can give it our best shot and try to overcome these problems.

Acknowledge what has gone wrong and what is going wrong but try not to dwell on this as it is now time for you and your dog to overcome these concerns.
Being positive at this point can really help and yes, sometimes this will be difficult!

Replace 'I want to CHANGE my dog's behaviour' to 'I want SHAPE my dog's behaviour'.

Remember it may not only be your dog's behaviour that needs modification.
You may need to consider how your actions could be influencing the way your dog behaves.

Formulate a plan of action. This should start with a visit to the Vet to ensure there are no medical reasons for the behaviours you are concerned about. A behaviourist may also be an option if you feel you need extra help or for some of the more extreme concerns such as aggression.

Using the mental image of 'shaping' rather than 'changing' a dog's behaviour is an important key to achieving your goals.

be dependent on you for guidance and to structure his day.

Before you bring your new dog home, you will already be aware of what you would and would not like him to do in and out of the home. You may already have been given some information on your dog's behaviour in a previous home

BE REALISTIC: A DOG IS A DOG

Remember, no matter how much he seems to understand or behave like a naughty child, your dog is a dog, and he behaves like a dog. Dogs can be loyal companions and affectionate friends, but when things do not go to plan we can very quickly become disappointed.

In order to effectively shape the way he is behaving, you need to be realistic.

The first step was to remove the cause of the potentially aggressive signals: once the hands were taken away the dog gave a very different response, and was happy and confident sitting.

This dog appears to be giving some potentially aggressive signals, with her teeth clearly visible as a result of being handled.

She is now confident for some low grade handling. This was achieved by gaining her confidence and observing the reasons for her responses.

or in the re-homing centre. This can be extremely useful, as you may be able to anticipate this behaviour and therefore intervene before it takes place. If not, there is no need to worry, as this is a new start for your dog, and his reintroduction to a home and family environment is governed by you. This is true whether it is your first re-homing or your fifth.

In order to effectively manage and modify any unwanted behaviours you need to approach the issue without any preconceptions. Look at your dog's behaviour with an analytical eye. A positive mental attitude is essential. You must also try to feel confident that you can help him to behave in a more desirable manner. Using the mental image of 'shaping' rather than 'changing' his behaviour is an important key to achieving your goals. This means you will realize you are getting somewhere when he manages even a small part of what you want, rather than feeling defeated because he has not managed the whole behaviour in one go.

EXAMINING BEHAVIOUR CONCERNS

The key questions to ask about any behaviour that concerns you are: when and where does the dog behave in this manner? What does the behaviour consist of? These questions will help to identify the causes of the behaviour. Take note of his behaviour right from the start, especially any which seems abnormal, or which interferes with your daily life and routine. Even small details can be very important in developing a picture of what is going on. Once you have the answers to these questions you can ask the question 'Why?'.

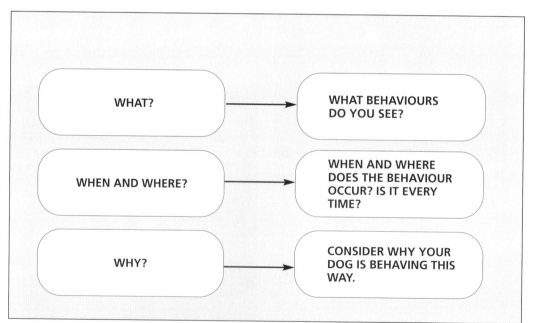

The key questions to ask about any behaviour which concerns you are: when and where does he behave in this manner, and what does the behaviour consist of? Then you can ask 'why'.

Why is he Behaving this Way?

Behaviour does not occur in a vacuum: all behaviour is the result of some motivation. By identifying this motivation we can gain the answers necessary to formulate techniques for progress. We can change the dog's drive to perform a specific behaviour by eliminating negative emotions or inducing alternative positive emotions, or we can remove the reinforcer.

Evolutionary Origins of a Behaviour

Why would dogs have a certain behaviour in their repertoire? The answer to this question gives a clue to understanding. For example, members of the *Canidae* family, such as wolves and dingoes, use scent marking by urination in the wild to indicate the boundaries of a territory – and even a happy, well adjusted dog may do this in a new home. However, if this becomes excessive then you will look for the cause in issues of territory. The evolutionary origins of the behaviour give you a starting point and help you to focus on the types of concern that a dog may exhibit.

Mind Map of a Behaviour Concern

It is sometimes difficult to answer a question when we are in a situation where emotions may be running high. A mind map is a quick and easy way to record all those competing memories, and will help you to pinpoint common features. Look at the example below and see if you can answer the key questions: what, when, where and why?

TECHNIQUES TO HELP SHAPE YOUR DOG'S BEHAVIOUR

The use of punishment and negative reinforcement can exacerbate a dog's problems, increase his fear, and may well make his reaction a great deal worse.

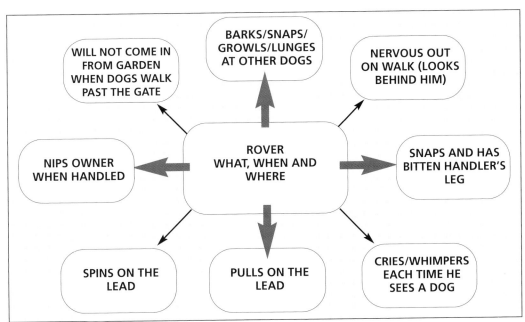

A mind map is a quick and easy way to record competing memories, and will help you to pinpoint common features.

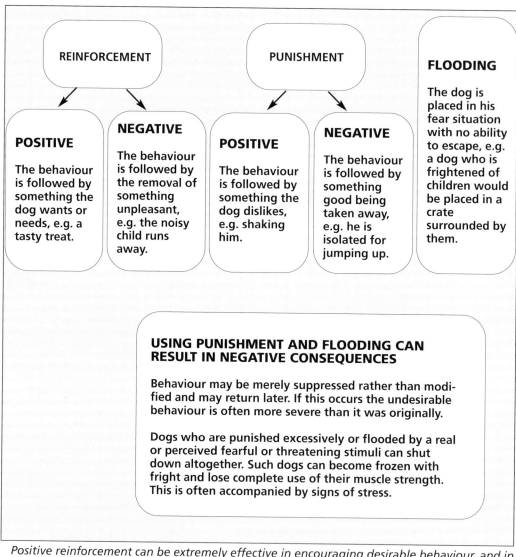

Positive reinforcement can be extremely effective in encouraging desirable behaviour, and in shaping behaviours that need modification.

Positive reinforcement, however, can be extremely effective in encouraging desirable behaviour, and in shaping behaviours that need modification.

Positive Reinforcement: Clicker Training

The idea of using positive reinforcement might appeal enormously, but you may have tried this in the past with limited success. If this is the case, then help is at hand, as over thirty years ago people began using the principle of positively reinforcing behaviour with sound linked to a reward. It began with marine animal trainers using whistles, and eventually reached the world of dog training where the whistle was replaced with the clicker (a small box that makes a clicking noise when pushed).

The clicker is superior in its effectiveness in marking desirable behaviour because the quick, sharp noise is easily recognized by the dog, and when paired with a treat becomes exceptionally powerful. The treat you use is entirely up to you; however, we recommend using very small amounts of food for each treat – the tastier the better.

Our voices can get lost in a dog's mind, as he hears talking throughout the day with huge variation. When the clicker is introduced as a positive reinforcer, it unmistakably signifies to your dog that he has done something correct. When a food reward is paired with the clicker sound, the dog not only recognizes he

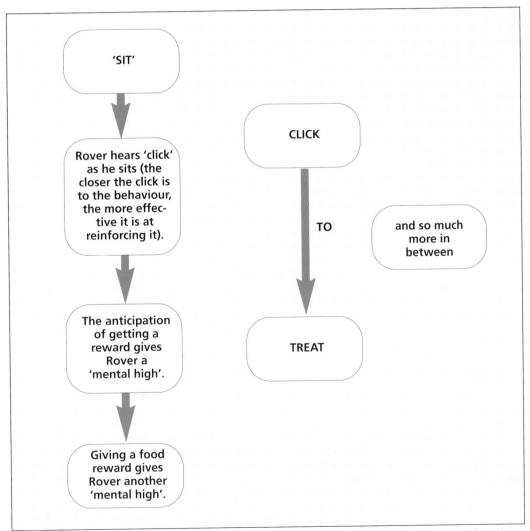

The clicker, when paired with the reward, unmistakably signifies to your dog that he has done something correct.

has done something right, but experiences additional positive reinforcement as his brain releases a chemical reward, dopamine, in anticipation of a treat. This is sharply followed by a further shot of dopamine as he receives the treat.

How the Clicker Works

The clicker is an extremely effective tool in shaping behaviour because not only does it give the dog a clear message that he has done the right thing, but in addition the consequent release of endorphins supports positive emotions. This means that it can be the key to unlocking any of the behaviours you thought were untrainable.

This is especially true for dogs with behavioural concerns. The clicker is a tool to help you train your dog more effectively and efficiently while making him feel good – though remember that you can positively reinforce behaviour by being positive and rewarding with praise: don't be afraid to do this if a clicker is not to hand. Also remember that if your dog is not particularly food-orientated you can use toys such as balls as his reward. This can work just as effectively, and many official search and sniffer dogs are trained this way.

Introducing the Clicker

Before you begin clicker training, you must ensure your dog is not afraid of the sound. If he is, then you may be doing more harm than good if you use it straightaway, as it will become a punishment rather than a reward. If he is concerned, it will take time to remove his fear: do this gradually by using a very quiet clicker to begin with, or by dulling the sound in a jumper or coat.

If your dog is not afraid of the noise you can begin 'clicking and treating'. This can be achieved by throwing a treat on the floor and as he gets close to the food, 'click' and he then will eat the treat. Repeat this until your dog connects the click sound with food.

The next phase involves giving your dog simple commands, preferably ones he already knows, and each time he follows the command correctly, click and treat. Repeat these commands a couple of times and you are not only reinforcing these behaviours, you are also teaching the dog that the sound of the clicker means he has got it right. Keep these sessions brief with regular breaks as your dog needs to experience consistent success, which will not happen if he becomes bored or loses concentration.

OTHER USEFUL TRAINING TECHNIQUES

Quite often training is impeded because a dog may be too stressed to concentrate on learning a new behaviour or even cope with the added pressure. A highly stressed dog can hear you, but is unable to listen as the adrenalin pumps round his body. Equally an excited, hyperactive dog cannot learn because he cannot concentrate. This means that if you can help your dog to remain calm you will have a much higher chance of shaping undesirable behaviour.

A relaxed dog is a receptive dog, and knowing how to reduce or remove stress is a valuable skill for any dog owner. In this section we offer you three techniques which have proved effective in helping a dog to remain calm and combat stress: the calm programme, mat training, and the 'watch me' command.

CALM PROGRAMME DEVELOPMENT

When Champ, a black labrador cross, arrived at the Dogs Trust Newbury re-homing centre he was suffering from severe stress. He could not settle even when taken into a quiet room, and demonstrated several stress behaviours. The most prominent of these was pacing behaviour, with whines and cries and sleep problems. Communicating with Champ was very difficult as he was too stressed to hear and found it very difficult to concentrate, let alone learn new things or cope with his new environment. As sleep is a key core need, its lack can cause additional stress and psychological concerns.

Vanessa began to wonder how she could shape his behaviour to help him feel more relaxed, in particular to lie down in a relaxed position. She began by offering treats low down so that he would have to lie low to get them. While he was reaching for a treat she would encourage him to rest his head as low as possible, at times on her lap.

Only minutes after lying in this position he stopped the vocal behaviour, closed his eyes and fell asleep. This was the first time Vanessa had seen him relax since his arrival a week before. As the 'calm' training developed he began to stretch his legs out behind him and his body followed, stretching out, and leading to the relaxation of his muscles. As time went on, the previous stressful behaviours were significantly reduced and he began to cope much more effectively with the kennel environment.

The Calm Programme

The principle behind the calm programme is that it is impossible to be relaxed and tense at the same time. When your dog is alarmed, the autonomic nervous system is activated and prepares him to run away or fight. Once the stressor is removed, the para-sympathetic nervous system takes over and lengthens and relaxes the muscles. This can be especially useful if you have a dog that is very excitable or prone to stress and anxiety.

The programme works by training the dog to adopt a position that automatically engages the para-sympathetic nervous system, and consequently will help him to feel calm and relaxed. Never force the dog into this position, as this would have the opposite effect by causing his muscles to tense, and could be potentially hazardous.

How to Train the Calm Command

- The starting point is 'sit'. Use 'click and treat' to teach this command unless he already knows it.
- The next step is to use a treat to guide the dog from sitting to lying. Use the command 'down' with click and treat. Do not manoeuvre him into the position with your hands as this is very invasive and not conducive to relaxation.
- When your dog is lying down, use the 'calm' command and repeat it while offering a treat to guide his head lower. The aim is to have the dog as low and relaxed as possible – his legs can be stretched out and he can be lying flat out on his side. There are many variations depending on the individual: some dogs will not like to lie flat out, so use your judgement to determine your dog's calm position.
- Feed treats as low as possible, below the level of the heart, to help to relax the body and therefore the mind. Click and treat regularly so that he is constantly positively reinforced for shaping his behaviour to this command, and is also learning that being with you is a pleasurable experience.
- If you feel resistance to the command, don't worry, but take a step back and try again later. Just standing in one

The dog is lowering his head and body into a down position, following the hand guide.

The dog is displaying the second stage of the calm command. The hand guide is still present, but his eyes are beginning to relax. Stop using the clicker at this stage.

The hand begins to move away and the dog stretches into a comfortable position and relaxes further. Note the change in expression, with the eyes becoming even less focused and the body falling into a fully relaxed position. At this point stay with him until he relaxes further, then take a seat close by his side.

place and focusing on you for thirty seconds can be beneficial for dogs that find being still difficult. As your dog begins to reach a higher level of relaxation, stop using clicker reinforcement as this can keep the dog alert and prevent him from relaxing completely.

Mat Training

Mat training is an additional method for building relaxation and concentration. You can train your dog to associate the mat with safety, a place where he can feel at ease. This means that you have a useful tool to calm your dog when visiting friends, or when you have to take him with you on more serious occasions.

The mat itself should be made of a warm material that is both comfortable and comforting for the dog. Fleecy materials are good, and a thermo backing is ideal so that the cold of the floor cannot strike through. You can also move a mat around to various locations when you are trying to build stationary training.

THE EMOTIONAL BENEFIT OF WARM MATERIAL

The ability of soft, warm fabric to comfort an animal was demonstrated in the fifties by Harry Harlow in his research on deprivation in infant monkeys. One group of monkeys received food from a wire-covered substitute mother, the other from a 'mother' covered in soft towelling. When both groups were frightened by a mechanical toy, the group with the cloth-covered 'mother' clung to her, but the other group threw themselves on the floor, rocking backwards and forwards under considerable stress. Thankfully, this unethical experiment would not be allowed today, but it has been observed that dogs derive emotional benefit from warm material, and if given a preference will choose mats of this type over materials such as rubber or even the bare floor.

How to Train the Mat Command

Once again it is important that you do not manoeuvre your dog with your hands, but shape his behaviour so he understands what is required. Shaping has the added advantage of being an effective mental exercise for your dog. But remember, little and often – take a break after five to ten minutes, or if your dog is starting to lose concentration.

- The aim is to teach your dog to have a positive association between the mat and safety.
- The mat should be large enough for your dog to lie on without spilling over the edges.
- First reward him for being near the mat, or for touching it with his nose or feet. Achieve this by guiding him to the mat giving the command 'mat', and click and treat when he puts a paw in the right location.
- Repeat this exercise until he has effectively understood the principle – that is, when he goes to stand on the mat at the command 'mat'. Now you can use the command 'sit' when he is standing on the mat.
- Continue with 'mat', click and treat, then 'sit', click and treat, until he goes to the mat and sits without the command 'sit'.
- Make it easy for your dog to learn this command by standing in front of the mat to begin with. Use the word 'mat' while standing further away, and reward him for going to this area.
- Then begin to increase the distance you are standing from the mat when you give the command. Looking or pointing at the mat will help to communicate what you want him to do.
- You can then ask your dog to lie down on the mat and see if he can learn to reach the mat and then lie down. Although many dogs can pick this up quickly, there are those who do not, so take it slowly, with frequent breaks.
- Never punish your dog if he does not do as he is asked: this would defeat the

Giles is displaying how to sit correctly on his mat.

As the mat training develops you will be able to increase the distance you can leave your dog.

purpose of the exercise, as you are trying to teach him how to relax. This can only be achieved by using positive reinforcement along the way.

- The next stage is training your dog to stay on the mat area. This begins by asking your dog to 'stay', and then pausing for a couple of seconds, and if he has remained still, click and treat. If instead he jumps up or moves, ask him to do something simpler, such as sit on the mat. You can then click and treat. This will also help to develop the command you are trying to teach. Once again, don't worry if he doesn't get it first time. The training is supposed to be fun and enjoyable for both of you.

- Once you can get him to 'stay' for a couple of seconds, begin increasing the time, from three seconds to four to five, and so on. At this point stay in the same place and do not move away from him. When he can stay on the mat for thirty seconds, you can begin increasing the distance you are from him. This is harder, as your dog may really want to be with you, so move only one step away at a time. Click and treat every time he does what you are asking. Once again, if he doesn't do what you ask, go back to a step he can do, and reward him.

If you begin asking for the 'watch me' command while standing still it enables the dog to focus more easily. Giles is displaying a 'watch me' while sitting down, which is a good position for him while he is taught the behaviour.

The 'Watch Me' Command

The principle of the 'watch me' command is to focus your dog's attention on the handler. This is very useful if your dog becomes agitated by something in the environment when you are out and about, and it has the additional benefit of simplifying lead work. By training him to 'watch' you at any stage in a situation that concerns him, you can change his troubled emotional response to a calm one. For example, if you know that bicycles worry your dog, then as soon as you see one approaching you give the 'watch me' command, and this redirects his attention from the bike on to you.

This command is very useful in the counter conditioning process, which is a method whereby you substitute one behaviour for another. As the dog learned the 'watch me' command when he was calm and relaxed, he will associate the action with this state. In other words, in the case of the bicycles, you are conditioning him to be calm and relaxed in the presence of cyclists. Eventually this state will replace his previous fear so he will no longer feel the need to bark anxiously as a cyclist whizzes past.

How to Train the 'Watch Me'

- Start the training in a quiet location with few distractions. The garden is a great place to start as your dog knows where he is; it is contained and you can limit the distractions.

- While your dog is on the lead, pick a moment when he is looking elsewhere to say, 'Watch me'. Use a friendly tone in a higher pitch than normal, and as he looks at you, click and treat.
- Take a few paces forwards and ask again. If he responds, click and treat once again.
- Before you take him out to another location, ensure he responds to the command when you are walking around the garden.
- Progress to new locations but only those that are reasonably quiet. This is because a distracted, stressed or fearful dog has difficulty hearing you as his attention is totally focused on the point of concern.
- On each walk, limit your use of the command to two or three occasions; this will ensure he remains responsive to the word. If he does not respond, it is likely that he is too excited by the environment to 'hear' you. Move on and ask again when you know he is less involved in what is going on around him. Slow the pace or stop to make things easier for him if he is finding it difficult to learn. As with all training, it should be carried out when you have the most chance of success.
- Aim to achieve the 'watch me' command while walking along, and to get even brief eye contact while still moving.

The 'watch me' can be a fantastic tool to take a dog's attention away from a possible fearful stimulus. This means you can reward the calm behaviour and support the reinforcement of positive emotions around the source of concern, thus reduc-

The 'watch me' can be a fantastic tool to take a dog's attention away from a possible fearful stimulus.

ing or eliminating the concern.

With practice his response to this command will become 'automatic'. Furthermore, in a situation that your dog finds stressful, he may even turn to 'watch' you when you have not asked him to; this would show that you had successfully modified your dog's reaction to anxiety-provoking stimuli.

MENTAL EXERCISES AND FUN GAMES

Dogs have evolved to live in a complex environment to which they must be able to adapt in order to survive. Therefore, dogs have the ability to think and solve problems, such as how to reach the deliciously smelling field mouse at the bottom of its hole, or how to scale a fence to get to another dog. Although living with humans has removed the necessity to find food, we have replaced this with the necessity to work. We have bred dogs to herd, hunt, track, retrieve

Dogs need a rest after both physical and mental activity.

THE RULES OF ENGAGEMENT

Most dogs need an exercise session in the morning and early evening. Mental training sessions and games, however, can be structured at any time throughout the day as long as the dog is eager to participate. Bear in mind the following 'rules'.

- Keep the sessions short and fast-paced. For some dogs, three minutes is enough; other dogs concentrate for six or seven minutes.
- If your dog is having trouble, get him to do a trick you know he can do easily so that you can end the session on a high note.
- Stop playing before he gets bored.
- Have frequent breaks so that he will then need to refocus his attention on you.
- If he starts to get over-excited, take a break: when dogs get over-excited, it is difficult to train them as they find it harder to concentrate.

and guard, and these traits exist at some level in even the most mixed-breed dog. This has left dogs with a continuing need to exercise their skills, and without an outlet they can become destructive, anxious or frustrated, causing numerous concerns.

Providing mental exercises for your dog has several benefits: it not only provides an outlet for his skills, but also strengthens the bond between you. A dog that is used to problem solving will be more able to cope in a variety of situations – essential if something goes wrong. Mental exercises also keep him from getting bored and destructive, because after a session of these, he will be content to just settle down on his own for a well-earned sleep!

In the early days of your relationship with your rescue dog, you will be discovering what he already knows and filling

If your dog becomes over-excited, it would be wise to have a break.

- Play a variety of games to keep things interesting for both of you.
- Make at least one of the games an aerobic activity, as this will release endorphins that help him to keep calm.
- Remain positive and keep it fun; whatever happens, don't lose your temper or shout at him.
- One new game/trick/command per week is more than enough, but not all dogs learn at the same pace so don't feel frustrated if it takes two weeks or more instead of one.
- A dog easily forgets if he is not given opportunities to practise, so continue with old tricks/games even when he has learnt new ones.
- The quickest and easiest method for teaching your dog a new trick is to use what your dog does naturally, for instance lying on his back. Link this with a word and a treat, and you have your first trick. By clicking and treating natural behaviours while using a command word you can reinforce any behaviour you would like to.
- Teach your dog something within his capabilities and nature. Determining the capability of a pure-breed dog is straightforward, but there are usually identifiable features in a mixed-breed dog. Trial and error is one way forwards, as long as you are not grittily determined to stick with the trial and deny the error!
- Remember that anything that involves your dog's attention is a mental exercise.
- If your dog suffers from frustration, avoid games which may add to this. 'Find it!' games could be a little too much for some and must be played at a low level. Every dog is an individual, so judge each situation independently.

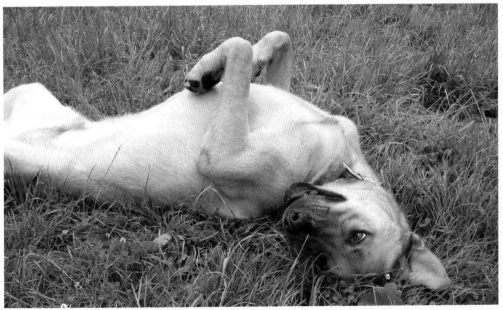

This dog is lying on his back of his own accord. Click and treat while using a command word, and you can reinforce this behaviour.

This dog is mid-way through performing a spin on command.

distances or the number of items involved.

In the photograph (left) the dog is midway through performing a spin on command. Bear in mind that although training this type of command for many dogs is fun and a good use of their mental and physical abilities, it is important not to reinforce this behaviour if the dog displays it without prompting or when it is stereotypical.

Games and Tricks

'Speak!'

Every time your dog barks or makes a noise, praise him whilst saying 'Speak!'. Eventually your dog will 'speak' when asked.

Paw

When your dog is sitting, say 'paw,' and take his paw gently with your hand. Praise or treat him, then let his paw go. Do this a few times every day, and after a while say 'paw,' but do not take his paw. See if he raises his paw by himself. If not, keep showing him what to do by saying 'paw', and taking his paw with your hand. He will get the idea eventually and when he does, praise him lavishly!

Hide and Seek

This is a good mental game, as your dog must use his senses to track things down; you can play this indoors as well as outdoors. Tell your dog to 'stay', and then when you are out of sight call him to you. Either use your normal 'recall' command or just his name, and praise him excitedly when he finds you. You can then make it more difficult by 'hiding' behind trees and sheds, or indoors behind doors or furniture.

in the gaps. Start with short sessions (five to ten minutes), making sure your dog receives lots of praise and rewards so he has fun. Once he can respond to the basic commands of 'sit', 'down', 'stay', 'come', you have the foundation for much more interesting possibilities. Moreover, in the process of this training you will have established an understanding with your dog: he will know that if he can figure out what you are asking him to do, he will get a treat of some kind. As the training continues, physiological changes will occur in his brain, as a consequence of which his mental capacities will actually expand.

Eventually over time, you will be able to cut back on the rewards until your dog will respond to just the hand gesture or verbal command such as 'speak' or 'fetch'. However, vocal praise should always be used. Once a new trick is secure in the dog's mind, you will be able to build on it, for example by increasing the

Touch Target

Teach him to use his nose to touch anything: hand, foot, touch stick or household item! To teach this, give a command such as 'touch hand', while offering your hand; as he touches, reward him. By teaching your dog to touch target objects such as a touch stick, he can learn to follow this item and do new tricks: spin, under legs and even stand up!

'Find It!'

'Find it!' is another game to play indoors or out. First get him to sit and show him a treat. Tell him to wait, or get someone to hold him, and walk a couple of steps before placing the treat on the floor. Go back to the dog and say 'Find it!', and let him go. When he gets to the treat, praise him and let him eat it. This teaches him to associate 'finding' the treat with the command 'Find it!'.

Over the next few days increase the number of paces before asking your dog to find the treat. Once he understands 'Find it!', which can take minutes or days, increase the difficulty. Let your dog see you placing the treat half hidden from view behind a piece of furniture. Once again ask him to 'Find it!'. When he succeeds, praise him. Gradually make it more difficult, but stick to one room.

Once he 'finds it' reliably in the same room, hide the treat in an adjoining room. Get him to use his nose by letting him sniff your hand before you ask him to 'Find it!'.

Once the principles of this game are established, a whole world of possibilities opens up.

Tracking

You can try a variation of the 'Find it!' search game in your local park. Use your dog's ball or a small piece of cloth. With your dog on the lead, walk to a quiet spot, and while he is not looking, drop the ball or cloth. After a few paces stop, turn round, say 'Find it!', and walk in the direction of the ball or cloth, encouraging him all the time. If he doesn't find the ball himself, point to it, give him plenty of praise and play the game again.

The Shell Game

Now you can move on to a much more challenging game. This is a variation on that old sleight-of-hand trick performed by conjurors. Take three heavy cups, buckets or receptacles, which will need some effort to overturn, and place them face down on the floor. Ask your dog to sit, and let him watch as you place a treat under one of the 'shells'. Say 'Find it!', and as soon as your dog shows that he knows which 'shell' covers the treat, either by pawing or even just standing next to it, then give him the treat and praise him.

Repeat this process by switching the 'shell' the treat is hidden under. Once he grasps the rules you can space the 'shells' further apart, or add more 'shells'. Do not turn the 'shell' over until he finds the one that actually contains the treat.

Find 'Keys'

Once you have practised the shell game for a while, you can teach your dog to do something really useful: find your keys! Attach a small piece of cloth or leather to your key chain, and rub this well so that the material absorbs your scent. Next, repeat the shell game with your key chain instead of a treat, and the word 'keys' instead of 'it'. When your dog finds the 'shell' that hides your keys, lift it up to reveal your keys, give him lots of praise and a treat.

Finally, leave the 'shells' and start hiding your key in other places around the room. Start by placing them where he cannot miss them, but eventually he should be able to sniff them out in places such as fruit bowls, drawers and on tables.

The 'Name Game'

It is possible to build an association with the name of an object. Select two very different items such as a ball and a rubber bone: by calling each one by its name when the dog plays with it or fetches it, he will slowly begin to understand which item it is.

To play this game, say 'Find the ball!', and bounce the ball so your dog pays attention to it. When he touches the ball, say 'Good ball!' and give him a treat. The next stage is to lay it on the floor next to the bone and repeat 'Find the ball'. Praise and reward him when he touches the

It is possible to teach the dog to build an association with the name of an object.

ball. If he touches the bone, swap it for the ball.

This is obviously a very difficult game for your dog as he has to be able to identify different sounds and to connect them with an object. This makes it very tiring, so this game should be kept very short.

Eventually, increase the number of items so your dog will be able to pick the ball from among several items.

'Tidy up!'

Collect your dog's toys, or some objects you don't mind him handling, and scatter them in a small pile on the floor. Say 'Tidy up!', and by giving him clear messages, such as pointing towards the items, encourage him to pick them up one at a time, and place them in your hand. You may have to resort to exchanging one item for another in order to get him to give you what he has picked, and reward each item with a food treat, and then drop it into a waiting box. Some dogs may start putting things directly into the bucket themselves.

'Fetch!'

'Fetch!' is a favourite game for many dogs. Use a ball that is not too small to swallow, nor so hard that it damages his teeth.

One of the basic methods of training the 'fetch' command is to use two of your dog's favourite toys. Show him one of the toys, and then throw it a short distance. Say 'Fetch!', and hopefully he will chase after it and pick it up. When he starts to return with the toy, say 'bring it back', and produce the other one ready to throw for him; like this he is likely to drop the toy he has in order to chase the other one.

Keep the distance you throw the toy short, as this makes it easier for the dog to keep it in sight and remain concentrated.

Eventually you will be able to cut back on the rewards until your dog performs the trick with just the hand gesture or verbal command such as 'Fetch!' or 'Go get!'. And once the new trick is firmly lodged in your dog's head, you will be able to build on it, for example by increasing the distances or number of items involved.

Puzzle Toys

There are lots of toys on the market that are specifically designed to mentally stimulate your dog. These involve some easy puzzles, which the dog must manipulate to get to an edible treat. As they tend to be variations on this theme, you can make your own versions. The shell game can be adapted so the treat is placed inside one of several cardboard boxes: having identified the correct box, your dog must then work out how to get to the treat. The main thing to remember is that any container used must be made of a material that will not splinter or poison your dog.

It is easy to set up an obstacle course inside or outside the house, and have fun teaching your dog to find his way

Giles is poised ready to play with this very large ball.

through it. A rugby ball as opposed to a normal ball is an interesting alternative as the shape makes it unpredictable when rolled, and your dog will find this an engaging activity. Different size toys can be very challenging and fun for dogs to play with.

14 COMMON CONCERNS

In this chapter we deal with some of the common concerns that owners may face with their dog's behaviour. Quite often what is a behaviour concern to one person may be a source of amusement for another. Titch, the Jack Russell terrier, makes his owners very happy when he jumps up on the sofa for a cuddle, but it would be quite another matter if Max the Great Dane adopted this habit. There are, however, some behaviours that universally cause concern irrespective of individual lifestyles. Early recognition of a behaviour that is likely to develop into a concern makes it easier to intervene and help change your dog's actions before the behaviour becomes habitual.

If your dog has already developed undesirable behaviours do not give up hope, as there are still things you can do to shape the way he acts.

IN THE HOME

Separation Anxieties

The severity of distress shown when dogs are left by their owners can vary a great deal. The root of the distress, however, remains the same: insecurity. Insecurity is often the result of attachment concerns. Possible causes are: adverse events in puppyhood, such as early separation from the mother, loss of an owner, limited human contact while left alone for long periods of time; even a change in environment such as a move to a new house can create insecurity.

How to Help

It can take many months for a dog with severe separation anxiety to overcome his concerns, although a lot can be done to influence his behaviour. As the anxiety often stems from your dog's insecurity about your relationship, you can do several things to make him feel more secure. Clearly you should spend as much time as possible together, and some of this time should be used in interacting with him. If possible try to take some time off so that you can conduct the training gradually; this will make it easier for both of you. The very act of training on a daily basis with plenty of positive reward is therapeutic in itself, because in the process you are bonding with each other. Include the calm programme and mat training: the calm programme will help to reduce stress, and the use of the mat will be a tool to increase his feelings of security.

Many dogs suffering from separation concerns have insecure attachments with their owners: in such cases building your relationship is the way forwards. You need to reduce your dog's insecurity about being left alone, as this is the key reason why he is distressed by your absence. The most successful way of achieving this is to remain with your dog as much as you can for the first few

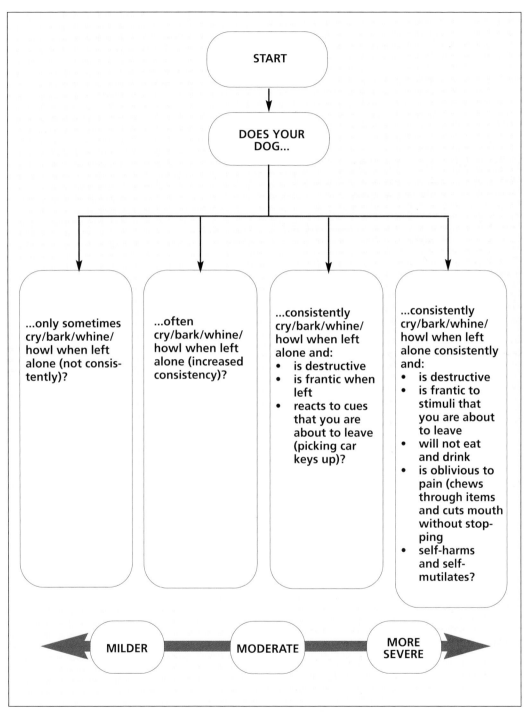

Full 'separation anxiety' is very severe, and many dogs suffer from milder concerns generated from anxiety from being left alone.

weeks of training, and to desensitize him by gradually building up the time you can leave him alone.

Begin by using the mat in the room where you will be leaving him, and ask your dog to wait while you take steps away. Continue until he can cope with you going out of sight. If you begin desensitization with the door open, you are already taking one of the major anxiety triggers out of the equation. Once he is confident waiting in the area for a few minutes you can begin to close the door, but always return after a second or so and reward him for waiting.

It may help to place his crate (always kept open) in his 'safe' room, and line it with one of your sweaters, which will smell comfortingly of you. Leave him in this room for a few minutes at a time while you are still in the house. This can work very well alongside the calm training and a great deal of positive reward. If it is possible, leave a radio on while you are away, as many dogs find this calming. However, he should be frequently exposed to the radio before you leave him so that he does not develop an association between the radio and the anxiety of being left.

Before you leave him, make sure he has had some exercise followed by a meal, and the opportunity to go to the toilet. This should help him settle down before you leave, and to sleep while you're not at home. Even if your dog has already eaten before you leave him, it is still advisable to leave him with a tasty chew, as chewing things can help calm a dog. If your dog is anxious, avoid rubber toys filled with food or treats he has to work to get, as this could add to his frustration. A better alternative is a large bone or pig's ear, which he can easily pick up and chew with no added stress.

Randomize where you position the treat and vary the times you place it in his calm room, so there is no danger of building up an association.

When you arrive back home after he has been on his own, it is vital that you do not ignore him, as this will only add to his anxiety and insecure attachment.

However, as the aim is to show him that your absence is no big deal, avoid giving the impression that he has done something amazing by being left alone: calmly greet him and continue with your routine. Whatever he may have done while you were away – been to the toilet on the carpet or destroyed the cushions – do not tell him off. He will not know why you are angry with him, and will now have an additional problem in that you

HOW TO LESSEN THE STATUS OF ANXIETY-PROVOKING CUES

Some dogs become anxious at the sight of their owner preparing to go out, and it is often helpful to lessen the status of these cues; this can be done by adapting the following schedule to your own routines.

Prepare to leave the house: get your coat, keys and so on.

Go to the door, and do not show your dog that you know he is upset (if you do, he might assume this is the reason for the next step). Do not leave the house, take off your coat and wait a few minutes.

Then get ready to leave again. Go to the door, open it for a few seconds, and then close the door, take off your coat and wait a few minutes.

After a few minutes, repeat the process, but this time go outside and close the door; wait for thirty seconds. Go back inside, take off your coat and carry on as normal.

Repeat this every day, taking more time between each step until you can stay outside for a few minutes without any reaction from your dog.

make him unhappy when you go away, and you shout at him when you come back, so your leaving him is a really, really bad thing.

Reluctance to Give Up Items

If a dog does not want to give up whatever he is holding in his mouth, in your efforts to wrest it from him, his mouth and teeth may be dangerously close to your hand. Offering a substitute toy is a much safer and more effective way to retrieve an object from a dog's mouth than going to grab it.

What To Do

- The secret is that you do not take anything from the dog without giving him something in exchange.
- Do not punish your dog if he does not want to give up an item. Punishment will add to his concerns and will

This dog does not want to give up his ball, and his mouth and teeth are dangerously close to the hand.

destroy his confidence. It will make him less likely to want to come near to you, let alone give you his favourite ball. Punishment will only teach him that he cannot trust you, and that you will punish him if he lets you get too close.

- In order to train your dog to give up items you can start with swapping whatever your dog has for something of equal, if not greater appeal. If you are trying to play 'fetch' when your dog has a ball and does not want to give it up, pick up another ball and show it to him as if you are going to throw it. When he becomes interested, throw the ball and he will drop the one he already has so that he can chase and pick up the other.

- This technique can work in different situations. Imagine your dog has your child's doll. Instead of snatching it off him you take a tasty treat or one of his own toys and hold that out to him. Once he has dropped the doll, praise him and give him his own toy. In this way he learns, through positive reinforcement, that it is better to give up an item rather than hold on to it.

- Swapping an item is effective because you are replacing one desirable object with another. Not only is this a much more agreeable manner of obtaining what you want, but it teaches your dog that you are not likely to steal from him. Swapping items is helpful for dogs that are very protective of their possessions because they learn to trust you not to take them away. This helps them to gain confidence, and the resource becomes of much less importance.

Mouthing

Mouthing is a common concern and can

vary from a dog lightly holding and nibbling hands and arms, to holding tightly and firmly or grabbing any part of a person's body. The intention behind mouthing is different from that behind biting, although the difference between the two can become a little indistinct and it is, therefore, never desirable. Dogs use their mouths on one another in play, particularly as puppies, although many adult dogs also display mouthing actions. Many rescue dogs have been through a great deal of change in their lives, and those that come into a rescue early in their life may have had their puppyhood foreshortened through the experiences that have happened to them. Some of these dogs undergo a 'second puppyhood', and owners are faced with a two-year-old-dog acting like an eight-week-old puppy! This is a good sign, because it shows that the dog is feeling increasingly positive and

the expression of suppressed behaviour is very healthy. However, even in these cases, mouthing behaviour is not desirable.

Dogs that are suffering from stress can also resort to mouthing, especially when being handled, as stress makes their skin particularly sensitive and uncomfortable when touched; other dogs might be unaware that this behaviour is undesirable as their previous owners may not have discouraged mouthing in the past. The fact of the matter is that it is just not acceptable to have a dog using his teeth on any part of your body, crucially because he is unable to distinguish between play mouthing with his male owner and play mouthing with your three-year-old daughter. The best option is to avoid it happening in the first place, so discourage your dog from using his teeth at all. Remember, prevention is better than cure!

What To Do

- First you need to know why he is mouthing. This can be achieved through observation in order to answer the what?, when?, where?, why? questions.
- There are several possible reasons for mouthing. If it only occurs when he is playful perhaps he is simply a little rough. Mouthing people who are trying to handle him suggests that he is stressed or has some anxiety about being handled. A dog that is stressed commonly reacts to touch or restraint, but this behaviour may also stem from negative experiences in the past.
- It is vital that every member of the family or household is consistent in the training approach. It only takes one person to ignore or encourage your dog to mouth, and the behaviour will

Giles is mouthing his owner's hand in this photograph. As an adolescent, he can get carried away while playing, so using a toy to focus his mouthing energy would help.

remain.

- Do not punish your dog for mouthing; simply train him to do something else. Punishment can make the mouthing a great deal worse and mutate into a more defensive display because your dog will be fearful of, or worried about you. This is especially true if he is already wary of being handled.
- Have a toy at the ready, and when he begins to mouth your arm or hand, offer the toy instead. When he accepts and mouths the toy, reward him immediately. This can work wonders for the dog which just wants to play with something, and clearly a toy designed for the purpose is going to be more satisfying than your arm!

Jumping Up

Dogs that jump up on people are a common concern for many owners and their visitors. When a dog is excited and pleased to see you he wants to gain height to be as close to you as possible, but this is not compatible with keeping all four feet on the floor. Not only are dogs inadvertently likely to scratch and hurt people when they jump up, but people who are nervous of dogs can be quite alarmed when a dog jumps up at them.

So many dogs jump up, but can your dog sit on command? If not, teach him to sit, as it is extremely difficult for dogs to jump up if their bottoms are on the floor. For greyhound owners out there, 'stand' will suffice, but the dictum 'Four feet on the floor' is fundamental to this whole process.

What To Do

- Every time you feel your dog is likely to jump up at someone, ask him to 'sit'. Ensure that all the people involved

Teach your dog to sit on command, as he can't jump up if his bottom is on the floor.

with him reinforce this by not encouraging him to jump up.
- Use 'click and treat' to train your dog to sit at the feet of visitors rather than jumping all over them.
- Do not punish or push your dog down or away when he jumps up. He may be pleased to see you, and pushing him away shows him that you do not share his pleasure. If your dog has an insecure attachment with you then it is even more vital that he is not pushed away. In addition, the physical action of pushing a dog away with your hands actually encourages jumping up, as handling him, even if it is in a negative way, can reinforce the jumping up behaviour.
- Instead have a treat at the ready, lure his nose into a sit position, and reward him when he does just that.

House-Training Concerns

Vanessa once received a phone call from a gentleman who was having considerable problems with his four-month-old puppy urinating and defecating in the house. The problem was severe, with the puppy toileting on the sofa and all over the house. What was interesting was that the puppy was totally house-trained when the owners were not present!

The owner admitted to losing his temper with the puppy on several occasions, punishing her every time she went to the toilet in the wrong place. As a result the puppy had become so nervous that the ensuing anxiety led her to toilet whenever they were present. When it was explained to the owners that punishing a dog for toileting in the wrong place was the cause of the behaviour, they stopped and the puppy's concern almost instantly improved.

There are various emotional reasons such as fear and stress to explain why a dog may toilet in the house. However, there are also three basic explanations with equally prosaic solutions:

- Your dog could not hold himself: do not leave him alone so long, or take him out to the toilet before you leave him.
- Your dog does not understand where he is supposed to go to the toilet. Go back to basics and teach him the essentials.
- If he consistently urinates indoors, he may be incontinent. Take him to the vet.

Whatever the reason, naughtiness is not one of them, and as it is not a crime, punishment is inappropriate. It is a common misconception that punishing a dog for toileting in the house is the correct thing to do. Punishing on discovery of a pile of mess on coming home from the shops will make your dog behave in what appears to be a 'guilty' manner on your arrival, but does not mean that he understands why you are angry. It certainly does not mean he will understand that he is supposed to go in the garden.

In order to successfully house-train your dog you have to positively reinforce toileting in the correct location, rather than waiting for it to go wrong. Every time your dog goes outside, you go with him. As soon as you see him go to the toilet you praise him, then he will know he is being praised for going to the toilet. It will take more time for him to realize the praise is only given when he goes outside. Although it is easier to train a young dog to toilet outside, it is still quite possible with an adult dog that is not already trained.

What To Do

- Have a command word for toileting behaviour, such as 'toilet'.

ACCIDENTS WILL HAPPEN – CLEANING TIPS

If you use a product that contains ammonia to clean up your pet's urine, you won't be able to smell remaining odours, but your pet will! In fact, dogs have a highly developed sense of smell and will still be able to smell their own urine even if you have mopped it up with an ammonia-based cleaner. This means that the dog may continue to urinate where he has made mistakes before. The answer is to buy a special enzymatic cleaner developed for cleaning up pet accidents. Your supermarket should stock these cleaners.

- Show your dog or puppy the area you want him to use as a toilet using the 'toilet' command. Stay with him in this area until he has gone to the toilet, and give him a great deal of praise when he goes ('click and treat' works here, too).
- Take him into this area frequently at first (every ten to twenty minutes for a puppy, and every hour for an adult).
- If you see him sniffing or circling in the house, take him out straightaway.
- If he does toilet in the house, do not punish him. Ensure you clean up the mess thoroughly so no scent remains, and try to keep a better eye on him next time! If he toilets when you are out or overnight, the same applies.
- Dogs are extremely reluctant to toilet in the area where they sleep or eat. You can use this trait when you leave him alone by ensuring he is in a small area of the house, such as the hallway or kitchen, along with his mat or bed.

This dog appears to be having a great deal of fun digging the plants out of the pot. However, there can be many reasons for destructive behaviour.

Chewing and Destructiveness

Destructive behaviour tends to be directed at any number of possessions, such as shoes or toys to carpets, sofas and even doorframes. Dogs can do a great deal of damage in a relatively short space of time. Vanessa once came home to find her five-month-old puppy ripping the stuffing out of her sofa cushions. She had only left him for half an hour and this was the result! Destructive behaviour is often linked directly to separation anxieties, although adolescence and boredom are other possibilities.

What To Do

The solution to overcoming this behaviour lies partially in management and partially in training.

- First of all you should limit the possible damage by removing any items that you would not like to be chewed.
- Secondly, when you go out, leave him in an area such as the kitchen or hallway where he can do minimal damage. Make sure that the doors to all other rooms are shut so that things of value are not at risk to little mouths and teeth!
- Always have plenty of toys and chews available when you are with your dog and when you leave him alone.
- If he spends most of the day on his own, he may be bored. Reconsider your dog's mental and physical exercise regimes. Are they sufficiently challenging so that he is ready for a rest when he has completed them?

OUT AND ABOUT

Pulling on the Lead

We have all seen dogs that take their owners for a walk. Pulling on the lead can be an embarrassing and aggravating concern for many dog owners, and arises from one fundamental principle: putting a lead on a dog effectively teaches him to pull. This may sound rather odd, but the fact of the matter is that dogs learn to lean against the lead in order to get as quickly as they can to their destination.

Let us also remember that a lead is a very unnatural device for a dog and prevents him from walking the way he might choose to if he had the freedom do to so. Anybody who has watched dogs off lead in a park is likely to have seen them running backwards and forwards, walking or trotting along in all directions. Many young and healthy adult dogs would not choose to plod along at the exact pace of their owner because that is not their natural gait. We must therefore be sympathetic to our 'natural' dog and encourage him through training to adopt 'our' technique – remembering, however, that it may not be as easy for him as we imagine!

Training starts with how you, on the other end, respond to his pulling: to counter this behaviour you should not jerk or wrench the lead when your dog pulls as this just encourages him to pull harder – instead you should use the lead to gently guide him.

Try the following to see how it works: ask somebody to pull your arm, and you will find it very difficult not to resist and to pull against them. Now get them to guide your arm firmly but gently: this makes it much easier to move in the direction intended by the person guiding your arm. Now relate this to your dog's neck: which is going to be more effective, painful pulling or gentle steering? Pulling generates tension and frustration in both you and your dog; it may also make you angry, which in turn could make you want to punish your dog.

Teaching your dog to walk loosely while on the lead takes patience, practice and consistency. Many people give up too soon because they take their dog to a busy park and wonder why he does not listen and is not walking close to their legs. As with all training it is essential to build the behaviour gradually, which is easier to do when there are fewer distractions. When you feel the command is adequately reinforced, move on to more challenging locations, but do this in small steps. As we have discussed earlier, small steps are so much easier to accomplish and more enjoyable, as each step gives you and your dog a sense of achievement.

What To Do

The best way to train your dog not to pull involves no pain or punishment, but relies on teaching your dog a different relationship with the lead.

- Begin the training in a place with no distractions, not even a destination! Start in the garden without a lead, which makes it more fun for your dog and more relaxed, as no coercion is involved: he is choosing to be with you.
- Encourage your dog to walk close by your side by holding a treat. In a cheerful tone say 'heel', and if he responds, reward him with a 'click and treat'.
- Take a walk around the garden practising the command while there are few or no distractions. Walk in circles, and if your dog begins to wander, guide

Giles is walking to heel without a lead: note his relaxed and happy expression, showing he is enjoying the training.

To 'super train' his heel work, give your dog plenty of positive reinforcement throughout this training.

him in this circular direction. Give lots of positive reinforcement when he is by your side and ensure you give him regular breaks to enable him to concentrate effectively.

- The next phase is to reintroduce the lead while still in the garden. Hold it loosely, and practise the 'heel' command, continuing to click and treat the desirable behaviour.
- When your dog understands the command and it is becoming automatic, take him on the lead out of the garden to a quiet location. This could be a park at a quiet time of day. The quieter the area, the easier it will be to maintain your dog's focus on developing loose lead walking. If he begins to put tension on the lead, use large circles to guide him in the right direction.

When your dog understands the command and responds automatically, take him on the lead out of the garden to a quiet location.

- When he no longer pulls on the lead you will be able to go anywhere with him as you will be taking him for a walk and not vice versa!

Refusing to Go for Walks

A concern that occurs most often with nervous or under-socialized dogs is that once outside their own territory they refuse to go any further. Such dogs are so anxious about the world outside their home that they simply freeze. Putting them on a lead and trying to pull them into action just adds to their concern.

Other dogs are quite happy to run about when they are off the lead, but will refuse to move as soon as the lead goes on. This is very significant, as it shows they do not feel safe on the lead: the lead takes away the dog's ability to fight or run away if afraid.

What To Do

- As with the problem of the dog pulling on the lead, start in the garden. Encourage him with treats to walk by your side in circles around the garden. Reward even small steps, and keep the session short. If he is reluctant to move, get him to respond to his favourite squeaky toy. This will teach him that walking with you is very rewarding.
- The next step is to use the lead while walking round the garden. Don't forget to use plenty of praise.
- When you eventually risk the area outside your garden, put him on the lead (in case he surprises you and runs away), stand in front of him and call to him. If he refuses to move, wait as long as you can and if he makes only a slight movement towards you – click and treat. Make sure you do it while he is moving, not after he has stopped or before he has started. If you cannot manage this, try luring him with a tasty treat, wave it under his nose and as soon as he moves, click and give him the treat.
- Gradually increase the number of steps between clicks.
- Once he is able to walk some distance with you, make sure you keep him at a safe distance from anything that worries him, and circle away if you need to.

Biting or Ragging the Lead

This can be extremely aggravating behaviour! A dog that holds the lead with his teeth and hangs on to it, often ragging and pulling against the owner, is a potential hazard for both the dog and owner. A dog can very easily injure its mouth when engaging in such activity, especially if its teeth catch any metal buckles or fastenings. This is one reason to avoid chain leads. In addition, 'lead raggers' commonly get very close to their owner's hands when holding on, in their attempt to get greater control over the lead. The motivation behind such behaviour can stem from stress or frustration, or it may even have been taught or encouraged in the past.

What To Do

- Never encourage your dog to play tug or rag, or even pick his lead up with his mouth. The lead is not a toy or an item to play with. Do not fight with your dog when he rags the lead, nor pull against him: this is likely to make him think it is a game, and make the activity even more enjoyable for him. Avoid playing tug-of-war games with such dogs for the same reason. Have a toy at the ready and encourage him to hold on to this instead.
- If your dog is not interested in the toy,

make fitting the lead an exercise in itself; use your clicker and treats to break the process into stages. If he is frantically jumping around, ask him to sit, wait, clip the lead on, and off you go, clicking and treating as he succeeds with each command. Once again punishment is likely to make the complaint worse, especially if the root of the cause is stress or frustration.

- If your dog has become a habitual 'lead ragger' while out on walks, use a toy to divert him. Ensure that the toy you use for walks is separate from all his others, and ensure it is something he loves to carry. By redirecting the 'ragging energy' you can successfully modify such behaviour. In addition, giving simple commands can encourage the dog to focus and become calm through the release of dopamine in the brain, actively retraining the behaviour.
- If your dog is a very determined 'lead ragger', using two leads can be another useful method. Clipping on two leads, or using the double-clip lead in the manner described earlier, and dropping whichever lead he begins to grab, avoids your unwilling participation in such activities. You will have to be quick for this to work, however.
- If you are out in a field and your dog is ragging the lead and you have no tools to help you, stop moving and wait until he stops before going anywhere else. Always reward him when he drops the lead, however exasperating it is!

Other Concerns with Dogs on the Lead
A large proportion of the concerns people have with their rescue dog's behaviour involve walking on the lead.

Owners describe their dogs lungeing, whining, screaming and barking, while one lady said her terrier did a 'flymo' manoeuvre at the sight of another dog! Most of this unwanted behaviour occurs at the sight of an external stimulus such as other dogs, traffic, cats, people or livestock. The dogs become so stressed that they are unable to concentrate or focus. Some owners even feel that their dog is having an attack of some sorts as the dog seems oblivious to everything but the 'stimulus'. Effectively this is not far from the truth as their dog is experiencing the effects of a surge of adrenalin triggered by the 'fight or flight' response.

What To Do
- Before you can take action you must first identify the stimulus, namely what causes the behaviour to occur.
- Having identified the stimulus, you then need to desensitize the dog to it.

In spite of the ponies in the field, this dog is responding perfectly to the 'watch me' command. Note how the handler is smiling and making eye contact with him; she also has a treat in her hand at the ready.

Do this by exposing him to the stimulus from a safe distance: this will be some what further away from the distance your dog normally begins to react to the stimulus.

- Use the 'watch me' command to keep him calm and focused, and reward him with 'click and treat' when he complies. If he begins to react to the stimulus, you are too close and he cannot yet cope with this level of proximity. Take him further away by leading him in a curve, a more gentle movement than simply turning back. Then regain his attention with the 'watch me' command.

Recall

Trust is an essential component of the relationship you have with your dog, and one of the foundation stones to this is his returning to you when called. Nothing is more distressing than the thought that you have lost your dog as you call frantically for him. Some dogs may not return when called because they are just too busy nosing around in the undergrowth even to have heard you; others do not return because they know there is no need to come first time because you will keep on shouting until they are ready. Some dogs think that the voice you use means that you are angry with them, and if you are standing with your hands on your hips they are probably right!

The most important factor in training recall is that you ask your dog to come to you in a cheerful and friendly manner. Shouting or punishing your dog because it has taken him twenty minutes to return to you will not make him want to come back the next time. It may be frustrating and cause you anxiety and concern, but grit your teeth and put him on the lead, praising him as you do so: in this way he learns that something good happens when he returns.

Here is a dog on a mission, oblivious to the two ponies on either side of him. At times like these, when hazards are present, it is very important that your dog will come back to you on command. This can be a very difficult thing for a dog to do!

What To Do

- Build the recall command in a location where there are few distractions, such as in the garden. A volunteer is very useful during this stage, so recruit a helper if possible to be at hand.
- Ask the helper to stand next to your dog, taking the lead from you. Then ask your dog to 'wait' and walk a few metres away in front of him so he can see you.
- Then stand up straight, open your arms and smile and say 'Come' in a very lively, fun manner. If this word has failed to recall him in the past, then it is a good idea to choose a new word for this new training so that he has no inbuilt associations.
- As he runs to you, keep smiling and when he is close say 'sit', then 'click and treat'. Put your fingers through his collar to make sure he cannot run away. Never grab him as this could cause him to become fearful or defensive.
- Practise recall in the garden, and when you feel he is really getting to understand the command, move on to an outside area. Choose a place free from distractions, or take him there at a quieter time of the day. If the area is not fully enclosed and safe to allow your dog off the lead, a long line can be used. The same principle applies, but as you ask your dog to wait, the helper will hold the line and let out enough line to reach you when you call your dog.

UNIVERSAL PROBLEMS

Fear and Nervousness

Displays of nervous behaviour are common when rescue dogs arrive at their new homes, and in some instances the dog is also fearful. This can be due to several factors in particular, previous experiences. If you know that you have adopted a nervous dog, ensure that when he first comes home with you, he is entering a peaceful environment – no banging doors, noisy conversations, or attempts to play with him. Let him get to know his new home in his own time. Calming herbs or flower remedies such as Bach's Rescue Remedy™ may help him to relax. Put some in his water, but don't try to put it directly into his mouth as this will only alarm him. Some dogs have specific fears and it is often quite obvious what they are.

What To Do

- If you know the source of the fear, do not over-expose the dog to it. For example, if he backs away from a member of your family, ensure that this person does not try to touch or stroke him until he is more settled. Instead look for ways of encouraging him to feel less fearful and be more confident. For example, play simple ball games that he will enjoy, that will help him not only to relax but also to make positive associations with you and your family. But be warned, there are some dogs who either do not know what toys are, or are fearful of them.
- If you are uncertain as to the source of his fear, careful observation asking the 'when', 'where', 'what', 'why' questions is needed to identify it. Having done this you need to desensitize him to his fear object by presenting it at a low level that he can cope with, or if appropriate, from a distance. As soon as he shows stress or fear, take a step back. For example, if he is beside himself when the doorbell rings, find a way of muffling the sound and only

over some time increase the level. At the same time you should click and treat calm and confident behaviour when the bell rings.

- If your dog is fearful when getting into the car or during car journeys, the same principle applies. Break the experience into sections. Start with leading him to the car and then taking him back again without actually getting in. When he is confident with this, begin to open the door and so on. Use positive reinforcement throughout the process when he is achieving the desired behaviour. Never tell him off when he is showing a fearful response because he will certainly not want to participate – and who could blame him! Remember to do this in stages and take regular breaks. Ten minutes may be quite long enough to start the process.
- If your dog is frightened by infrequent events such as storms or fireworks, allow him to bury himself under the coats in your hall, or provide him with an old duvet he can burrow into. Surrounding himself with your comforting scent will be an additional bonus. If he hides in an inconvenient place such as under your bed, do not try to drag him out, as this will only heighten his fear. Above all, do not appear concerned! The last thing he needs is confirmation from his best friend that you are both in a bad situation!

Stereotypical Behaviour

Behaviour under this classification has no obvious function and is often compulsive in nature. Such behaviour, although commonly found among rescue dogs in the kennel environment, is much rarer in the home. This is because stereotypical behaviour is often the result of 'stress build-up' which, as we have explained, is rife among kennelled dogs. Behaviours such as spinning, wall licking, tail chasing, shadow chasing, whirling and other variants can fall under this classification.

What To Do

- Such behaviour in the home is concerning and it is important to take the dog to the vet for further investigation.
- Ensure you do not restrain the dog when he is displaying any of these behaviours, and once again avoid punishment as this will add to the concern.
- Try to determine any pattern to these occurrences and note when they occur, and any possible stimuli.
- Ensure you make the environment as relaxed as possible.

AGGRESSION

Aggressive behaviour can be understood as acts of hostility and physical violence. A large proportion of aggressive behaviour stems from fear, with frustration and other psychological components influencing such actions to a lesser extent. Aggressive behaviour can range from something quite mild such as a brief growl, to severe, such as full offensive biting. However, a warning can easily escalate into action, and that is what we, as owners, want to avoid.

Before we say more on this subject, we want to make it clear at the outset that modifying aggressive behaviour is not a recreational activity: if you have reason to believe that your dog could bite someone or something, then you must seek professional help as soon as possible, first

IDENTIFYING AGGRESSION

The following is a behaviourist classification system of aggressive behaviour in dogs: the behaviourist will ask you detailed questions about your dog's behaviour; the session may last a couple of hours. It will be useful if you record your observations in a journal under the following headings:

Date: Sexual status:
Name: Diet:
Age: Last vet visit:

- What caused the aggression?
- To whom was it directed?
- What behaviours were shown?
- When does the behaviour occur?
- What were the dog's postures at the time?

After the first meeting the behaviourist will devise a remedial programme as well as a professional opinion of the risk involved.

of all from your vet, and then from your re-homing centre. This is because there are plenty of medical reasons for aggressive behaviour: your dog may simply be experiencing pain, although other common causes include epilepsy and diabetes.

We refrain from giving specific advice about the modification of such behaviour because there are so many variables behind a possible cause, and without examining each case in great detail it is very difficult to offer a sound plan of action. However, we aim to give you a greater insight into the different types of aggression to enable you to be prepared for further investigation, offering you 'in the meantime' advice to help manage the situation if you have to wait for further help.

Types of Aggression

It is important to be aware of the 'types' of aggressive behaviour and the motivation behind them in order to be able to present as much detail as possible for further investigation.

Potentially Aggressive Signals

The most obvious indications of defensive and offensive aggression consist of direct snarling, growling, snapping, nipping, biting and lungeing. However, you should also be aware of the more subtle signs including freezing, staring, glaring, and showing teeth. These signals reflect how the dog is feeling and they should never be ignored; if these early signs are missed, then the dog may have to intensify his behaviour to clarify the message he is trying to convey. Fear is a likely source of many signals, as the dog displays such 'warnings' to make the 'aggressor' back off.

It is vital that you are receptive to these signs: stop what you are doing so you can take a step back and work out what was provoking this reaction. Engaging in conflict at this point can be very dangerous and will not help the dog overcome his concern. Remember, many owners believe that their dog became offensively aggressive without warning or provocation, while it is more likely that the dog may have been using these lesser signals for months. If you ignore, punish or suppress such behaviour you may put yourself in a much more serious position.

Fear-induced Aggression

Such behaviour can become apparent when people or other animals approach a fearful dog; it often occurs with dogs that are frequently or severely punished. It can be more intense if the dog is on the lead because he cannot run away, and it can be exacerbated if the owner is nervous, because the dog detects the ensuing adrenalin. In anticipation of a threat, the dog will tighten up on the lead and stiffen his shoulders. The tail will be down, and the weight will be on the back feet and not over the front feet, showing that the dog wants the one approaching to go away.

Fearful dogs will often display submissive body language. They may hold their ears back flat and will avoid direct eye contact. They may even perform submissive urination. Charmingly, they will lick hands and roll over to expose their bellies. However, if they are cornered, they are equally likely to snap or bite. Such dogs are often afraid of human hands and consequently dislike grooming or having their feet touched.

They may have an insecure avoidant, ambivalent or disorganized attachment status, and find it difficult to cope with being left alone.

DOG FIGHTS

There is no failsafe way of splitting up fighting dogs, and it is far better to avoid the possibility altogether. In some cases it might be possible to distract the dogs so they let go of each other and can be safely grabbed and separated. You could also try throwing water or a jacket over them, which just might disorientate them.

A possible consequence is that one or both dogs will set upon the person breaking up the fight. Even more possible is that in the highly charged situation your hand reaching out to separate the dogs may not be perceived as a hand, but part of the fight. In addition, the dog may redirect his frustration and charged emotion on to you. So be very careful and avoid getting in between fighting dogs whenever possible.

Predatory Chase – Predatory Aggression

This can be directed at many things including other dogs, cats, or anything that stimulates a chase response, such as bikes, skateboards, joggers and cars. The key factor is that movement is often the trigger. Although predatory behaviour occurs in dogs of any sex and age, those that show intense interest in the movement or noise of children or pets should be closely watched.

It can be difficult to modify this behaviour as it may be instinctive rather than learnt. However, aiming to focus the dog and encouraging him to keep adrenalin levels low can be very useful. The 'watch me' technique can work very well in helping owners with such concerns.

Frustration or Redirected Aggression

In human psychology it is known that frustration can lead to aggression, and not necessarily against the perpetrators of the frustration. Interestingly, there is some evidence that the same is true of dogs. A common cause of such aggression occurs when owners try to restrain a dog that is trying to display a particular behaviour, such as pulling towards another dog in an offensive manner; while a dog that is barking at a hissing cat may redirect his aggression on to the owner who is restraining him. Therefore you should ensure that you do not get between a dog and the target of his aggression.

Management in the Home

There are many dogs that show concern when strangers enter their home environment, for example the postman or indeed any delivery person. Such people arrive at random times of the day, often waking the dog from slumber with the crash and bang of items falling through the door. Often they leave just as the dog begins to bark, convincing him that the removal of this strange threat coincided exactly with his barks and growls.

Such experiences encourage the dog to believe he is able 'protect the home'. This is instinctive behaviour, but is more extreme in individuals that are insecure, nervous or fearful. Every noise can become a threat, and every knock on the door a considerable cause of anxiety, so before the door even opens, the dog waiting the other side is in a highly stressed state. Vanessa has seen many cases of dogs behaving very aggressively towards visitors when owners open the door and the dogs are allowed to rush out just as a surge of adrenalin peaks.

Many of these dogs are the most loving of individuals in the home, even towards the strangers once the dog has settled down; for others the fear only grows, with behaviour displays intensifying. Some dogs even begin to display stereotypical behaviour at this point as they become unable to cope with what is happening. Dogs that exhibit actual aggressive behaviour, or those who become a nuisance at the time of opening the door, make it very difficult for owners to manage the situation when visitors arrive.

The following management technique can be used to help dogs that are more of a nuisance than a threat to visitors' safety. It is also a useful interim technique to use while you are waiting for professional help with those who are either showing the potential to become aggressive or have already displayed such actions. However, it must be stressed that you should seek professional help with such cases.

The key to managing such situations is to train the dog to go to a different area of the house where he can be kept separate if necessary. This allows the visitor safe passage into the house. The aim is to shape the dog's emotional response from defensive and concerned to calm and relaxed when he hears the stimulus that signifies somebody is at the door.

It can be very useful to put a sign on the door to say 'knock gently, dog in training' to reduce the stimulus. If the door bell is the sound that really causes concern, it may be a good idea to disconnect it while you are training.

How To Do This
- Place the mat in a room where you can easily close a door, or use a stair gate to separate the dog from the entrance to the house. It is advisable to keep an aggressive dog behind a closed door, making it impossible for him to escape; a stair gate is only suitable for a dog that fits into the 'nuisance' category, rather than one that is a direct threat.
- Show your dog where the mat is, using treats guides or even his favourite toy, as explained in mat training (page 128–130). Ask him to wait, and increase the distance you can walk away before having to go back to him. Begin training this with an open door so that it is less intensive, working up to closing the separating door/gate as he gains confidence.
- Eventually, pair the sound of a knock or door bell with the mat command.
- Practise these sessions before anybody actually arrives, and use volunteers to walk round the house and knock on the door.
- Keep sessions short, just ten minutes at any one time; though depending on the dog's stress levels, you can practise this several times a day.

CONCLUSION

The process of re-homing a rescue dog can be a wonderful and fulfilling experience. The most important point for us to convey throughout this book is that a rescue dog is not a second-class citizen in the dog world, and that even in some of the most challenging cases you, too, can achieve success.

To find the right home for a rescue dog the re-homing centre needs to find the right match for a dog and new family alike, but the responsibility does not just lie with them. It is important that the entire family is involved in the process from start to finish, remembering that first visit appearances can be deceptive!

A truly successful homing requires the dog's whole family to understand behaviour in as much detail as possible: the 'why' is more important than the 'what' in many cases, especially when helping to change what may be going wrong. You can live in close harmony with your dog through understanding these situations and using kind and fair training methods to guide him along the way.

Offering a home to a dog without one is an extraordinarily rewarding exercise, and we often hear from the new homes of the most challenging cases that they find this doubly so. If you feel you can give a rescue dog a second chance, then you also get the opportunity to change both your lives for the better.

We leave you saying there is plenty more work to do.

Shadow waited many years in a rehoming centre before finding a loving home. There is an ideal dog for everyone – you just need to find them! (photo: Karen and Alan Kingswell)

FURTHER INFORMATION

REFERENCES

1 Siegel, J.M. (1990) *'Stressful Life Events and Use of Physician Services among the Elderly: The Moderating Role of Pet Ownership'* in Journal of Personality and Social Psychology

2 Hart, B.L. and Hart, L.A. (1985) *'Selecting pet dogs on the basis of cluster analysis of breed behavior profiles and gender* in Journal of the American Veterinary Medical Association (USA) 186(11): 1181-1185

3 Hopkins, S.G., Schubert, T. A., et al. (1976). *'Castration of adult male dogs: effects on roaming, aggression, urine marking, and mounting'* in Journal of the American Veterinary Medical Association 168(12): 1108-1110

4 Range, F., Horn, L., et al. (2009). *'The absence of reward induces inequity aversion in dogs'* in Proceedings of the National Academy of Sciences 106 (1): 340-345.

5 Wells, D.L., and Hepper, P.G. (1998) 'A note on the influence of visual conspecific contact on the behaviour of sheltered dogs' Applied Animal Behaviour Science 60(1): 83–88

6 Stephen, J.M. and Ledger, R.A. (2005) 'An Audit of Behavioral Indicators of Poor Welfare in Kenneled Dogs in the United Kingdom' Journal of Applied Animal Welfare Science 8(2): 78–95

7 Aloff, A. (2005) Canine Body Language: A Photographic Guide Wenatachee USA, Dogwise

8 Bortchelt, P. L. (1984) 'Behaviour development of the puppy in the home' in R.S. Anderson (editor) Nutrition

9 Tod, E., D. Brander, et al (2005) 'Efficacy of dog appeasing pheromone in reducing stress and fear related behaviour in shelter dogs' Applied Animal Behaviour Science 93(3-4): 295-308

10 McNicholas, J., Collis, G.M., et al. (2004). *'Beneficial effects of pet ownership on child immune function'*, 10th International Conference on Human-Animal Interactions, Glasgow

11 Vidovi, V.V., Šteti, V.V., et al. (1999). *'Pet Ownership, Type of Pet and Socio-Emotional Development of School Children'* in Anthrozoos: *A Multidisciplinary Journal of The Interactions of People & Animals* 12(4): 211-217. Wilson, C.C. and Turner, D.C., eds. (1997), *Companion Animals in Human*

Health, Enlarge image, SAGE Publications Inc.

12 Jalongo, M.R. (2004), *'The world's children and their companion animals: developmental and educational signif icance of the child/pet bond',* Olney, Mar: Association for Childhood Education International

13 Coppola, C.L., Grandin, T., et al. (2006). *'Influence of Human Interaction on Salivary Cortisol: Can human contact reduce stress for shelter dogs?'* Physiology and Behavior 87: 537-541

14 Aloff, A. (2005) *Canine Body Language: A Photographic Guide,* Dogwise, Wenatachee, USA

15 Beerda, B., M. B. H. Schildert, et al (2000) 'Behavioural and hormonal indicators of enduring environmental stress in dogs,' Animal Welfare 9: 49-62

16 Rugaas, T. (2006), *On Talking Terms with Dogs: Calming Signals,* Dogwise Publishing

17 Mech, D.L. (1999). *'Alpha status, dominance, and division of labor in wolf packs',* Canadian Journal of Zoology 77: 1196-1203

18 Belyaev, D.K. (1979). *'Destabilizing selection as a factor in domestication',* Journal of Heredity 70: 301-308

19 Coppinger, R. and L. (2004)

20 Daniels, T.J. and Bekoff, M., (1989). *'Population and social biology of free-ranging dogs, Canis familiaris'* Journal of Mammalogy 7(4): 754-762

21 Beck, A.M. (1975), *The ecology of 'feral' and free roving dogs in Baltimore.* The Wild Canids, M.W. Fox. New York, Van Nostrand Reingold Co.: 380-390

22 Topál, J., Miklósi, A., et al. (1998). *'Attachment Behavior in Dogs (Canis familiaris): A New Application of Ainsworth's (1969) Strange Situation Test'* in the Journal of Comparative Psychology 112(3): 219-229

FURTHER READING

Abrantes, R.A. (2005) *The Evolution of Canine Social Behaviour,* USA, Wakan Tanka Publishers

Fogle, B. (1990) *The Dog's Mind: Understanding your Dog's Behaviour,* Hoboken, N.J., Wiley Publishing, Inc.

Trut, L.N., Plyusnina, I.Z., et al. (2004) *'An Experiment on Fox Domestication and Debatable Issues of Evolution of the Dog Journal'* in Russian Journal of Genetics 40(6): 644-655.

WEBSITES

www.animalrescuers.co.uk
This site gives a list of over 30 breeds arranged in alphabetical order with a number of websites for each.

www.battersea.org.uk/dogs
Battersea re-homes dogs all over the country provided that you are able to collect the dog from one of their three sites: Battersea London, Battersea Old Windsor and Battersea Brands Hatch. If you live over five miles from the centre

you can fill in an application form online and a re-homer will telephone you in response. Those who live too far away for a home visit need to provide a letter of recommendation from a vet (or rescue centre).

www.bluecross.org.uk

The Blue Cross has eleven re-homing centres around the country. They promote responsible ownership and practical care of the animals they hope to re-home.

www.dogpages.org.uk

Dogpages is a non-commercial site run solely by volunteers. The aim of the site is to offer helpful advice and information across a wide breadth of dog-related subjects.

www.dogstrust.org.uk

The Dogs Trust is the largest canine welfare charity in the UK and has seventeen centres around the country including Northern Ireland. They have campaigned on dog welfare-related

issues for over a hundred years and go to great lengths to ensure their dogs go to a safe and happy home. They re-home thousands of dogs a year and provide owners with help at each stage of the re-homing process.

www.thekennelclub.org.uk

The primary objective of the Kennel Club is to 'promote in every way, the general improvement of dogs'. The Kennel Club was founded in 1873 and is able to offer dog owners an unparalleled source of information, experience and advice on dog welfare, dog health, dog training and dog breeding.

www.rspca.org.uk/rehoming

You can use these pages to look at some of the animals looking for homes and to find your nearest RSPCA in England and Wales. The adoption procedure can vary between RSPCA animal centres and branches. The best thing to do is to visit your local centre or branch and staff there will talk you through the process and help you meet your ideal dog.

INDEX